ENTREPRENEURIAL RESILIENCE:

INNOVATIVE SOLUTIONS FOR OVER COMING DISASTROUS CHALLENGES

A QUALITATIVE STUDY OF CHALLENGES, CONSERVATION OF RESOURCES THEORY, AND PATHWAYS TO RESILIENCE

By

Elizabeth Peters, PhD

Author's Note

This book investigated the gap in innovative, technology-driven disaster preparedness among Tennessee small to medium-sized enterprise (SME) owners—a shortfall contributing to premature business closures, job losses, and adverse economic consequences for the state. The lack of preparedness disproportionately impacts SME owners, managers, stakeholders, and incident response teams, with cascading effects on local economies and communities.

Guided by the Conservation of Resources (COR) theory, this study explored how Tennessee SMEs can adopt technology-driven disaster solutions to mitigate post-disaster challenges. Using a qualitative, exploratory case study design, the research employed semi-structured interviews with eight purposively sampled participants ($N = 8$). Transcribed data were coded, thematically analyzed, and validated through member checking to identify key barriers to implementing innovative preparedness strategies.

Findings underscored the critical need for SMEs to integrate technology-enhanced disaster resilience measures to safeguard organizational resources. Practical recommendations included:

- Establishing **effective communication protocols**,
- Implementing **targeted disaster preparedness training**,

- Leveraging **government-incentivized preparedness frameworks**, and

- Developing **dedicated incident response teams** with tailored readiness plans.

The study also highlighted avenues for future research, particularly in optimizing innovative, scalable disaster preparedness models for SMEs.

Acknowledgments

This milestone holds profound meaning as the first doctoral scholar in my family—a humbling testament to God's faithfulness. I am eternally grateful to the Almighty for His unwavering grace and strength. Jeremiah 29:11 has been my anchor: *"For I know the plans I have for you," declares the Lord, "plans to prosper you and not to harm you, plans to give you hope and a future."* You, Lord, are my Creator, Provider, and Sustainer. You knew the path ahead long before I took the first step, and your mercy carried me through every challenge.

To my National University (NU) Dissertation Committee—Dr. Ahmed Ben Ayed (Chair), Dr. James Webb (Subject Matter Expert), and Dr. Milton Kabia (Academic Reader)—thank you for your wisdom and dedication. Dr. Ayed, your steadfast mentorship and encouragement reignited my resolve during moments of doubt. Your guidance was the compass that kept me on course.

My gratitude also reaches the School of Technology and Engineering (SOTE) leadership, especially Dr. David Hildebrandt and Dr. Frank Appunn, for sharing their expertise and vision.

Finally, to the NU librarians, faculty, and staff: Your collective generosity, through resources, mentorship, and unwavering belief, made this achievement possible. This degree is not mine alone; it is a tapestry woven by countless hands. With a heart full of gratitude, I thank each of you.

Dedication

I dedicate this work to my beloved paternal grandmother, Mariam "Jaja"—your dreams of education were stolen by cultural barriers and early marriage, yet your spirit lives on in my pursuit of knowledge. How I wish you could see this moment, dear Jaja. To my maternal grandmother, Rosalie: your wisdom and quiet strength continue to light my path.

To my father, David "Papa": though the world denied you formal schooling in youth, you became a lifelong learner who cherished education's transformative power. Your belief in me was unshakable; I pray this achievement honors your memory. May your soul and those of my grandmothers find eternal rest. Your legacy of resilience carried me further than I ever dreamed possible.

To my precious family—especially my sons, Jake and Marc: you have been my anchor, my cheerleaders, and my reason to keep going. This milestone belongs to you as much as to me. Through every late night and weary day, your love reminded me why perseverance matters. Watching you grow into remarkable individuals has been life's greatest joy.

James 1:2-4 sustained me when the journey grew hard: *"Consider it pure joy...when trials come, for the testing of your faith produces perseverance. Let perseverance finish its work, that you may be complete."* These words—like your love— taught me that struggles forge strength.

Definitions of Key Terms

Business Continuity Management (BCM)

According to Asgary et al. (2020), BCM was defined as a preparedness framework organizations can implement to establish a robust and effective readiness and response posture to unexpected incidents or crises.

Business Resilience

Business resilience is a modern adaptation that organizations can implement to promote efficient business continuity (BC), emergency, and crisis management, aiming to mitigate disruptive events in business operations while improving DR capabilities from destructive incidents (Akpinar & Özer-Çaylan, 2023).

Cyberattacks

Cyberattacks are catastrophic incidents characterized by unauthorized access to an organization's data and technological systems, leading to disruptions in business operations (Sadeghi et al., 2022).

Disaster

Disasters are defined as severe calamities disrupting normal business activities, societies, or communities at various levels due to perilous occurrences, revealing vulnerabilities and risks, resulting in the destruction of businesses, loss of life and property, and adverse effects on economies (Sarmiento et al., 2019).

Disaster Management

Disaster management encompasses executing a framework for preparing against disruptions and adopting a pragmatic strategy for recovery (Akpinar & Özer-Çaylan, 2023).

Disaster Preparedness

Disaster preparedness involves overseeing and assessing a conceptual model or framework through established capabilities to address disruptive events impacting business owners and the workforce while ensuring operational continuity during crises (Verheul & Dückers, 2020).

Disaster Recovery (DR)

Disaster recovery is an essential process aiming to guide the re-establishment and rebuilding of businesses, adhering to organizationally developed incident response requirements to minimize the intensity of destructive impacts following a disastrous event (J. Ha et al., 2022).

Disaster Risk Reduction (DRR)

Disaster risk reduction (DRR) is a strategy directed at minimizing and recovering organizations from disruptions, outlining mitigatory objectives to lessen the occurrence of disruptive events and alleviate uncertainties and weaknesses to safeguard business resilience and minimize their impact (Sou et al., 2021).

Disruptive Events

Disruptive events span operational, managerial, and security setbacks, disrupting organizations' original performance, including natural hazards like tornadoes, fires, floods, and hurricanes (Akpinar & Özer-Çaylan, 2023).

Service-Dominant Logic (SDL)

SDL, described by Yogia et al. (2024), is about the convergence of services among organizations and is founded on digital operations, where consumers participate as co-creators of value through inventive and interactive means.

Small to Medium-Sized Enterprises (SMEs)

As defined by Utami et al. (2021), SMEs are organizations in the United States employing between 10-500 individuals while making a substantial economic impact on the nation. These enterprises typically possess total assets ranging from less than $100,000 to $15,000,000 and annual revenue growth between less than $100,000 and $15,000,000.

Technology-Driven Disaster Preparedness

Technology-driven disaster preparedness aims to utilize innovative resources like advanced data analysis, machine learning, and deep learning tools to predict disruptive events. This, in turn, assists business owners in safeguarding valuable assets and mitigating disaster risks (Hsu & Sharma, 2023).

Table of Contents

Author's Note i

Acknowledgments iv

Dedication v

Definitions of Key Terms vi

Introduction 1

    The Core Challenge 9

    Why This Book Was Written 11

    Theoretical Framework 12

    How the Research Was Conducted 15

    Research Objectives 18

    Benefits of this Research 21

Existing Knowledge and Gaps 26

    Case Study Strategies 27

    Guiding Theoretical Framework 28

    Corollary 1 32

    Corollary 2 32

    Corollary 3 33

    Corollary 4 34

    Historical Presentation of the COR Theory 34

    Indication of The COR Theory's Relevance to The Study 36

    Integration of the COR Theory 38

    Understanding the Current Thinking 39

    Historical Background of Disaster Preparedness & Understanding of New Technologies 46

    Sevier County Wildfires 47

    Historical Disaster Preparedness Management 48

    Challenges Hindering Disaster Preparedness 50

    Outcomes of Challenging Factors 52

    Consequences Of Unpreparedness 53

Disastrous Experiences 54

Technologically Innovative Disaster Preparedness Solutions 56

Maturity Model Exploration 59

Innovative Preparedness Policies and Frameworks 60

Government Agencies' Initiated Frameworks 64

Disaster Preparedness Training Initiatives 66

Enforcing Innovative Preparedness Training 67

Business Owners' Investment in Disaster Preparedness 70

Importance of Technology-Driven Disaster Preparedness 72

Workforce Disaster Preparedness 76

Risks and Vulnerabilities Mitigation Strategies 78

The Research Approach 82

Research Methodology and Design 85

Case Study Design 89

Exploratory Case Study 91

Alternative Qualitative Research Methodology Designs 92

Research Setting and Data Collection Method 94

Data Collection Protocol 95

Population and Sample 97

Detailed Description of the Population 98

Justification for the Sample Size and Sampling Method 98

Eligibility Criteria 99

Explanation of the Geographic Focus 100

Sample Population 100

Sampling Design and Size 102

Sampling Frame 103

Instrumentation 103

Semi-structured Interviews 107

Interview Process 108

Study Procedures 109

Data Analysis 111

Assumptions 116

Limitations...117

Delimitations 119

Ethical Assurances 120

IRB Approval Process...123

Key Themes and Observations..127

Trustworthiness of the Data...130

Results 136

Participant Demographics..142

Theme 1 SME Owners' Lessons Learned to Develop Mitigatory

Strategies...152

Theme 2 SME Workforces' Fostering of A Preparedness Culture 162

Evaluation of the Findings 174

Geographical and Demographic Limitations......................................177

Precision Geographical Limitations 177

Sample Size..178

Methodological Limitations 179

Trustworthiness and Validity...180

Research Findings...182

Implications, Recommendations, and Conclusions 188

Implications 190

Understanding Barriers Hindering the Integration of Preparedness

Solutions 197

Importance of Business Resilience 198

Integrating Emerging Technologies..198

Utilization of Rainy Day Fund (RDF) and Other Policies and

Frameworks 200

Collaborative Networks..201

Government and Nonprofit Support...202

Humanistic Approach to Data Collection 203

Technology-Driven Preparedness Training and Awareness..............205

Emphasis on Tailored Training Programs 206

Cultivating an Innovative Disaster Preparedness Culture 207

Impact of Communication on BC Planning 208

Investment in Technology-Driven Solutions 208

Strengthening Incident Response Workforce 209

Partnerships for Training and Development 210

Continuous Assessment and Improvement 210

Recommendations for Practice 211

Immediate Actions 214

Foster Collaborative Networks and Strengthen Communication

Protocols 214

Promote Business Resilience Through Training Development 215

Medium-Term Actions 216

Continuous Assessment And Improvement 216

Leverage Government And Nonprofit Resources 218

Long-Term Actions 218

Enhance Financial Support Mechanisms 218

Invest In Technology-Driven Solutions 220

Recommendations for Future Research 221

Adopting Disaster Preparedness Training 221

Preservation of Valuable Resources 222

Recruiting and Developing A Resilient Incident Response Team 223

Conclusions 227

References 231

Appendix A Research Instrument 256

Introduction

Implementing innovative disaster preparedness interventions is essential for Tennessee small to medium-sized enterprises (SMEs). Small to medium-sized businesses are organizations with 1–500 employees, whereby disaster preparedness interventions are vital for sustaining the business economies by integrating resilient strategies to withstand disruptive events (Asgary et al., 2020; Eggers, 2020). Small businesses constitute 99.9% of private sector organizations and 60% of employers, contributing 47% of business turnover towards the state's economy (Coates et al., 2019).

However, due to their size, financial constraints, and lack of technology-driven disaster preparedness, SMEs are particularly vulnerable to disruptive events, especially newly developed businesses (Eggers, 2020). This study highlighted concerns about the increase in disastrous events and SME owners in Tennessee's insufficient implementation of technology-driven disaster preparedness measures to mitigate crises (J. Ha et al., 2022; Palinkas et al., 2021).

Tennessee SME owners are challenged when implementing innovative disaster preparedness solutions against disruptive events due to numerous barriers and constraints that support them in several ways, one of which is financial resources to afford technology-driven readiness resources (Coates et al.,

2019; Kallmuenzer et al., 2024; Sarmiento et al., 2019). For instance, S. Ha et al. (2022) explained that in November and December 2016, several businesses experienced wildfires in Sevier County, which damaged over 17,000 acres, resulting in an economic loss of $500 million.

Additionally, the destruction impacted 2,400 buildings and 73 businesses, as S. Ha et al. (2022) continued to discuss, which led to the destruction of 14,000 homes and loss of lives. It must be noted that wildfires increasingly destroyed approximately 7 million acres of the United States' natural environment annually, doubling the original average of 3.3 million acres since 1990. Disruptive events such as wildfires continue to be concerning and are identified as hindrances to disaster preparedness by SME owners.

Reports at both state and national levels indicated increasing evidence of various disruptive events impacting SMEs, including weather occurrences, cyberattacks, and disease outbreaks (Asgary et al., 2020; S. Ha et al., 2022). The study indicates how disruptive events primarily affect SME owners by hindering business operations following a disastrous event, resulting in job losses and property damage. This, in turn, led to loss of life, revenue, and infrastructure (S. Ha et al., 2022). Furthermore, through the exploratory measures, disastrous events were identified to result in detrimental effects on SMEs, including inventory loss, equipment damage, data loss, financial setbacks, power outages, marketing services disruptions, and workforce displacement (Sarmiento et al., 2019).

Disruptive events include hazardous weather incidents, human-induced disasters, data security breaches, supply chain attacks, infectious diseases, and other elements (Asgary et al., 2020). These factors entailed incidents that emerged gradually or suddenly (National Institute for Standards and Technology [NIST], 2021). When SME owners experience disruptive events, the consequences are identified as severe and, in most cases, result in significant losses compared to larger organizations (Eggers, 2020).

Disastrous events have impacted SMEs' resilience, recovery efforts, revenue, and reputation, frequently resulting in business closures (Coates et al., 2019; J. Ha et al., 2022; T. Oyama et al., 2021). The outcomes of disruptive events are identified as being mitigated by adopting technology-driven disaster preparedness solutions and integrating effective strategies. Policies and framework integration were indicated to guide SME owners in adopting innovative and technology-driven disaster-preparedness solutions as readiness strategies (Coates et al., 2019).

Frameworks and policy effectiveness minimize the impacts of disruptive events while promoting efficient and expedited disaster recovery procedures. The absence of innovative disaster preparedness solution implementation by SME owners has exposed organizational vulnerabilities, which were addressed by integrating frameworks like business continuity management (BCM), contingency planning (CP), and disaster recovery (DR; Asgary et al., 2020; J. Ha et al., 2022). Integrating BCM within SMEs enables capabilities to facilitate organizational and operational management following a disastrous event and during the restoration of business operations to their pre-disastrous state (Q. S. A. Ali et al., 2023).

Small business owners promoted disaster preparedness by integrating disaster risk reduction (DRR) and BCM frameworks, ensuring business operations continued, emphasizing managing and enforcing disaster risk mitigation strategies with continuous residual risk monitoring (Sarmiento et al., 2019). In-house innovative disaster preparedness solutions included digital safeguards of essential data alongside the explored dependable backup methods from emerging response protocols adhering to DR, BCM, and CP frameworks, principles, and guidelines (Coates et al., 2019).

Business resilience procedures were promoted when SME owners implemented disaster preparedness solutions by integrating the BCM framework (Asgary et al., 2020; Coates et al., 2019). Small business owners' integration of the BCM framework was determined to maximize disruptive events' mitigatory capabilities and protect valuable business resources. Research indicated how the private sector, owned by SME owners, planned to establish policies and frameworks, such as BCM, DR, CP, and data security, to strengthen business readiness (J. Ha et al., 2022; NIST, 2021; Sarmiento et al., 2019).

The lack of BCM, CP, and DR was confirmed to extend SMEs' recovery timelines (Coates et al., 2019). In addition to policies and frameworks, SME owners' preparedness solutions have included training for pre- and post-disastrous readiness and documentation for all performance metrics (Q. S. A. Ali et al., 2023; T. Oyama et al., 2021). By integrating policies, frameworks, and training programs, SME owners can effectively mitigate disruptive events through technology-driven disaster preparedness solutions.

Training programs focusing on innovative, technology-driven disaster preparedness solutions, led by SME owners, enabled the workforce to adopt effective strategies for safeguarding business infrastructure, critical data, and vital systems against disasters (Coates et al., 2019; Gwon et al., 2022; Hobfoll, 2001; Seong et al., 2023; T. Oyama et al., 2021). These initiatives, by the Conservation of Resources (COR) theory principles, ensure a proactive approach that guides risk mitigation and resilience. Education for the workforce through training programs was a crucial element enabling the acquisition of practical preparedness response to disastrous events (Seong et al., 2023; T. Oyama et al., 2021).

According to NIST (2021), SME owners' adoption of innovative, technology-driven disaster preparedness strategies enabled the workforce to adapt procedures and establish a resilient business framework supported by structured training-based guidelines. On the other hand, the implementation of disaster preparedness training programs by SME owners stabilized business operations, enhanced resilience, optimized vital resources, and contributed to revenue growth, representing 50% of the nation's gross domestic product (GDP; Sarmiento et al., 2019; T. Oyama et al., 2021).

Future research should continue to build upon existing studies and documentation of lessons learned, highlighting the significance of SME owners implementing technology-driven disaster preparedness solutions (Sarmiento et al., 2019). This entails several key focus areas:

(a). Enhanced data collection and analysis: Building robust datasets, diverse SME owner experiences were captured during disastrous events, providing insight into the current preparedness strategies, including advanced data analytics to identify patterns, gaps, and opportunities to improve disaster response and recovery (Leary et al., 2023);

(b). Innovative Technology Integration: Exploring emerging technologies such as artificial intelligence, machine learning, and the Internet of Things (IoT) enhanced disaster preparedness and response capabilities through research to evaluate the effectiveness of these technologies in real-world scenarios while developing best practices (Shweta et al., 2022);

(c). Financial Resilience Strategies: Investigating in the role of financial instruments, such as disaster insurance, grants, and loans, in supporting SMEs' disaster preparedness efforts, whereby research continues to explore innovative funding mechanisms and public-private partnerships to improve financial resilience (Alisjahbana et al., 2022);

(d). Policy and Regulatory Frameworks: Examining existing policies and regulations related to disaster preparedness for SMEs and identifying areas for improvement, whereby research recommended that policymakers create supportive environments encouraging SME investment in disaster preparedness;

(e). Training and Capacity Building: Developing and testing training programs equipping SME owners and employees with the necessary skills and knowledge to effectively respond to disasters, where research can assess the impact of different training approaches on disaster preparedness outcomes (Gwon et al., 2022);

(f). Community and Stakeholder Engagement: Understanding the role of community networks and stakeholder collaboration in enhancing SMEs' disaster preparedness whereby researchers can explore how SME owners should leverage local resources and partnerships to build more resilient business ecosystems (Liang et al., 2023);

(g). Longitudinal Studies: Conducting long-term studies monitor the effectiveness of disaster preparedness initiatives over time. This can provide valuable insights into the sustainability of these efforts and their impact on SMEs' resilience to future disasters (Asgary et al., 2020).

By focusing on these areas, future research will contribute to developing comprehensive, evidence-based strategies to guide SME owners to better prepare for, respond to, and recover from disastrous events. This will support SMEs' long-term sustainability and resilience, benefiting individual businesses and the broader economy. Consequently, this study's research question is: How will Tennessee SME owners implement innovative and technology-driven disaster preparedness solutions to address challenges while preserving valuable resources?

This qualitative exploratory case study investigated how Tennessee SME owners have adopted or planned to adopt innovative and technology-driven disaster preparedness solutions to mitigate the impacts of disruptive events. Therefore, the study aimed to identify gaps in readiness posture continuing to pose challenges for SME owners in the face of disastrous events. Then again, the study was aligned with the COR theoretical framework, indicating principles encouraging SME owners to implement innovative and technology-driven disaster preparedness strategies to inform recovery mitigation strategies (Hobfoll, 2001).

During the study, semi-structured interviews were conducted with participants, consisting of SME owners, managers, stakeholders, and the incident response workforce, to collect data on implementing technology-driven disaster preparedness solutions. Participants offered insights into the technology-driven disaster preparedness solutions that are being implemented or considered to enhance disruptive readiness. The data collected from SME owners and managers revealed valuable lessons, illustrating how past experiences shaped business leaders' approach to disaster preparedness solutions, particularly regarding training, recovery procedures, and protecting essential resources.

The information obtained from the participants through the semi-structured interviews was analyzed for accuracy and generalizability. Keywords from the data were coded to filter the information and identify emerging themes. Additionally, the recordings of the interviews were coded and analyzed using NVivo 12 software to develop categories and themes.

The Core Challenge

The core challenge addressed in this book is that Tennessee SME owners face challenges when implementing innovative disaster preparedness solutions, which could often result in early business closures, job losses, and negatively affecting the state's economy (Coates et al., 2019; J. Ha et al., 2022; Sarmiento et al., 2019; T. Oyama et al., 2021). The challenges highlighted the urgent need to implement technology-driven disaster preparedness solutions, affecting organizational stability, revenue growth, workforce safety, business resilience, and reputation (F. Ali et al., 2023). According to the Centre for Research on the Epidemiology of Disasters (CRED), from 1998 to 2017, disasters that could have been anticipated resulted in 1.3 million deaths (Sarmiento et al., 2019).

The disasters affected 4.4 billion livelihoods and incurred economic losses totaling $2,908 billion, significantly depleting valuable resources. According to J. Ha et al. (2022), the consequences of inadequate preparedness included communication breakdowns, critical information breaches, supply chain disruptions, power outages, and property damage. These findings emphasized the need for research on how SME owners can effectively protect their valuable resources, guided by the principles of the COR theory (Hobfoll, 2001).

Without research to aid Tennessee SME owners in adopting innovative disaster preparedness solutions for disruptive events such as floods, cyber breaches, wildfires, and severe weather, businesses may be closed post-disaster (Green, 2023; Sarmiento et al., 2019; T. Oyama et al., 2021), resulting in workforce layoffs and significant revenue losses.

Future research should continue to investigate disaster risk mitigation strategies focused on adopting technology-driven solutions by SME owners (Hoerold et al., 2021; J. Ha et al., 2022; Q. S. A. Ali et al., 2023). Kallmuenzer et al. (2024) noted that the slow integration of innovative solutions was often due to inconsistent policies and inadequate resources.

Why This Book Was Written

The purpose of this qualitative exploratory case study was to examine effective measures of implementing innovative disaster preparedness solutions using mitigatory strategies against the challenges faced by Tennessee SME owners while strengthening organizational resilience. The study addressed the significant challenges Tennessee SME owners face in implementing innovative disaster preparedness solutions. Conversely, the challenges SME owners face have often led to early business closures, job losses, and negative economic impacts on the state (Coates et al., 2019; J. Ha et al., 2022; Sarmiento et al., 2019; T. Oyama et al., 2021).

The study underscores the urgent need for technology-driven disaster preparedness solutions to ensure organizational stability, revenue growth, workforce safety, business resilience, and reputation (F. Ali et al., 2023). From 1998 to 2017, disasters resulted in 1.3 million deaths and affected 4.4 billion livelihoods, causing economic losses of $2,908 billion (Sarmiento et al., 2019).

Inadequate disaster preparedness has been indicated to lead to communication breakdowns, critical information breaches, supply chain disruptions, power outages, and property damage (J. Ha et al., 2022). This emphasized the need for research on protecting valuable resources using the principles of the COR theory (Hobfoll, 2001). Without research to help Tennessee SME owners adopt innovative disaster preparedness solutions for events like floods, cyber breaches, wildfires, and severe weather, businesses may close post-disaster, causing workforce layoffs and significant revenue losses (Green, 2023; Sarmiento et al., 2019; T. Oyama et al., 2021).

Future research should focus on disaster risk mitigation strategies through technology-driven solutions by SME owners (Hoerold et al., 2021; J. Ha et al., 2022; Q. S. A. Ali et al., 2023). The slow integration of innovative solutions is often due to inconsistent policies and inadequate resources (Kallmuenzer et al., 2024). Moreover, addressing these challenges is critical to improving disaster preparedness among Tennessee SME owners, which will ultimately enhance business resilience and economic stability.

Theoretical Framework

The study used the COR theoretical framework developed by Professor Stevan E. Hobfoll (1989). This framework highlights the importance of safeguarding valuable resources for effective preservation. The COR theory is based on two key principles:

a) The loss of valuable resources negatively impacts the psychological well-being of business owners, managers, and investors, making it essential to regain lost resources.

b) The principle of prioritizing investments involves protecting existing resources from loss, recovering assets from any losses incurred, and acquiring new ones.

The theory is further elucidated through four corollaries: a) Corollary 1 recognizes a practical environment for resource investment; b) Corollary 2 explains that an initial loss of resources results in further losses over time; c) Corollary 3 suggests that resources gained early on lead to an increase in resources later; and d) Corollary 4 emphasizes the need to protect restored resources once damaged (Hobfoll, 2001).

The COR theory guides the exploratory case study and data collection methods by highlighting the benefits of SME owners adopting innovative disaster preparedness solutions to preserve valuable assets (Cai et al., 2023; Hobfoll, 2001; Pradhan et al., 2024). The COR theoretical principles and corollaries were incorporated into data collection interview questions to examine how disaster preparedness efforts aim to preserve valuable organizational resources. When critical assets or investments are destroyed, the resources acquired by SME owners are affected, leading to missed opportunities for revenue growth. These losses are classified as threats and failures within the COR theory, hindering revenue growth and creating additional burdens.

The study's findings underscored the importance of SME owners incorporating the principles of the COR theory as they took responsibility for implementing technology-driven disaster preparedness standards and procedures (Pradhan et al., 2024; T. Oyama et al., 2021). Ongoing research has further emphasized the value of the COR theory principles, offering insights into workforce autonomy as a key element in fostering employee readiness efforts (Pradhan et al., 2024). The COR theory views workforce insecurities as a form of resource loss (Pradhan et al., 2024).

By training employees to apply COR theory through established procedures and standards, SME owners help guide their workforce in safeguarding critical assets and data, thereby supporting business stability (Cai et al., 2023; Pradhan et al., 2024; T. Oyama et al., 2021). The COR theory served as a framework for the qualitative exploratory case study, highlighting the importance of SME owners protecting and preserving valuable resources, such as assets or investments, essential for business growth.

Overall, the COR theoretical framework emphasizes the importance of conserving valuable resources through various readiness principles (Sadeghi et al., 2022) and supports an effective research methodology and design for the study. Scholars have recognized the COR theory as a framework business owners utilize to implement effective strategies for safeguarding assets against disruptive events based on two core principles and four corollaries (Hobfoll, 2001; Pradhan et al., 2024). The critical need for SME owners to implement technology-driven disaster preparedness solutions points to a significant readiness gap in organizational readiness ability against disastrous events due to challenges SME owners face (J. Ha et al., 2022; Kallmuenzer et al., 2024).

How the Research Was Conducted

A qualitative research methodology was selected for this study as it aligns with the need to explore specific phases methodically (Bloomberg, 2022; Mohajan, 2018). Qualitative research focuses on narratives to understand lived experiences, which reveal lessons from different circumstances. Diverse data collection measures in natural settings, followed by qualitative data analysis tools, interpret and assess findings through words rather than numerical results (Mohajan, 2018).

The case study research approach was chosen for its ability to provide a detailed analysis of themes and lessons learned from specific cases, such as processes, events, or unique individuals (Bloomberg, 2022). This approach was prevalent across various disciplines, including education, business, and sociology (Tkachenko et al., 2022). It offers a robust method for exploring research questions narratively, often incorporating quotations to create a comprehensive storyline.

Case study research designs were versatile and used for theory development or testing, accommodating different methods of data collection and analysis (Tkachenko et al., 2022; Yin, 2018). This flexibility makes it suitable for exploring the unique experiences of Tennessee SME owners. Data collection involved semi-structured interviews with eight participants, including SME owners, stakeholders, and the incident response workforce, ensuring a diverse range of insights.

The study was conducted in the greater Nashville area, with pseudonyms used to maintain participants' confidentiality. Participants were selected based on their roles and experiences relevant to the research problem, ensuring diverse perspectives crucial for understanding disaster preparedness in SMEs. A sample size of eight participants was sufficient for providing rich, detailed data while maintaining a manageable scope for in-depth analysis.

NVivo software was used for data analysis, enabling systematic coding and categorizing of interview transcripts to identify themes and patterns. Its capabilities in handling large volumes of text and advanced querying functions ensured rigorous and comprehensive data analysis (Bazeley & Jackson, 2013). The study was guided by the research question: "How will Tennessee SME owners implement innovative and technology-driven disaster preparedness solutions to address challenges faced while preserving valuable resources?"

The study utilized a purposive sampling approach followed by randomization to facilitate in-depth data collection from the target population, thereby enhancing the research's credibility (Bloomberg, 2022). Random purposive sampling was used to achieve data saturation, with recruitment emails sent to random organizations in the greater Nashville area that had experienced a disastrous event in the last 2 years (Hennink et al., 2016; Keidel et al., 2021). The research identified factors impeding SME owners' adoption of technology-driven disaster preparedness solutions. Data were gathered through semi-structured interviews, transcribed using Otter.ai, and analyzed thematically using NVivo software.

A coding life-cycle approach was applied to define various construct procedures and generate sub-themes and themes (Kekeya, 2021). NVivo was utilized to manage and analyze the large volumes of qualitative data collected during the study. The software facilitated systematic coding and categorization of data, enabling the identification of patterns, themes, and relationships.

NVivo's advanced features, such as text search and query functions, allowed researchers to delve deeper into the data and uncover nuanced insights that might have been overlooked (Dalkin et al., 2020). Overall, NVivo played a crucial role in enhancing the qualitative analysis's depth, rigor, and transparency, making it a valuable tool for evaluating the collected data.

The study contributed to the literature by outlining procedures for implementing effective disaster preparedness solutions and establishing a transparent data collection protocol ensuring voluntary participation and confidentiality (Bloomberg, 2022; Mohajan, 2018). It emphasized data saturation, achieving a point where no additional themes could be developed (Hennink et al., 2016; Kekeya, 2021). This approach highlighted the importance of adopting innovative solutions to enhance SME resilience and mitigate disruptive events (Gennari, 2022; L. Karlı et al., 2022).

Research Objectives

The qualitative exploratory case study research questions were formulated as the basis for developing interview questions to collect data from SME owners through semi-structured interviews. These research questions were crafted to explore the lack of technology-driven disaster preparedness solutions implemented by SME owners to mitigate disruptive events. The case study was guided and examined using strategies to implement solutions to reduce the impact of disastrous events effectively.

Research questions were used to investigate how and which technology-driven disaster preparedness solutions SME owners adopted to improve organizational readiness and resilience. The research questions highlighted the significance of financial resources and policy development to mitigate the challenges outlined in the purpose statement, specifically by identifying the key barriers SME owners encounter when integrating digital preparedness technologies (Kallmuenzer et al., 2024).

On the other hand, the absence of integrated disaster response frameworks is seen as another barrier affecting the coordination of all departments and teams. Financial limitations consistently hindered SME owners from implementing technology-driven disaster preparedness (Coates et al., 2019; Eggers, 2020; J. Ha et al., 2022). The research addressed key gaps in the literature by examining practical strategies that SME owners could employ to overcome challenges and effectively preserve valuable resources during disasters.

The study aligned with the COR theory, underscoring the importance of safeguarding resources to mitigate the negative impact of valuable resource loss (Hobfoll, 1989, 2001). The sub-research question (R1a) specifically focused on the barriers and resource constraints that hinder the adoption of technology-driven disaster preparedness solutions. It explored how SME owners could overcome these obstacles, which are seen as threats to resource preservation, following COR principles (Hobfoll, 1989; Pradhan et al., 2024).

Another research question (RQ2) highlighted the need for cultural shifts within organizations to foster the adoption of innovative, technology-driven disaster preparedness solutions. This question is also connected to COR theory by investigating how a culture of innovation and technology-driven preparedness could enhance resource preservation and recovery (Cai et al., 2023; Hobfoll, 2001). The sub-question RQ2a tied to RQ2 addressed the practical application of the COR theoretical principles to enhance resource preservation integrated by SME owners for disaster preparedness.

Therefore, examining how SME owners should use the identified concepts to protect and recover resources during disastrous events, emphasizing the importance of resource conservation and the strategies needed to safeguard valuable assets (Hobfoll, 2001; Pradhan et al., 2024; Sadeghi et al., 2022).

RQ1

How do Tennessee SME owners implement innovative disaster preparedness solutions to address challenges while preserving valuable resources?

RQ1a

How do Tennessee SME owners integrate effective procedures to remediate challenging barriers or resource constraints that continue to hinder the implementation of technology-driven disaster preparedness solutions?

RQ2

In what way do Tennessee SME owners and incident response workforce embrace an innovative technology-driven disaster preparedness and solutions-oriented culture within their organizations?

RQ2a

How do Tennessee SME owners integrate COR theoretical principles and corollaries within organizations to preserve valuable resources by implementing innovative disaster preparedness solutions?

Benefits of this Research

The significance of this study was multifaceted, addressing theoretical, practical, and policy contributions while providing actionable implications for SME owners, managers, and stakeholders. The study indicated that the COR theoretical framework applied to the implementation of disaster preparedness solutions is a valuable resource preservation initiative by SME owners, filling a literature gap and enhancing an understanding of investment in conservation strategies (C. Wang et al., 2022).

Practically, the study detailed the importance of implementing innovative and technology-driven disaster preparedness solutions, emphasizing data-driven approaches to safeguard resources and enhance organizational resilience. Moreover, empowering SME owners effectively addressed disaster scenarios by integrating robust, resilient safety measures (Gennari, 2022; T. Oyama et al., 2021).

The study also underscored the importance of policy development to support SME owners, advocating for financial assistance, training programs, and incentives to adopt technology-driven measures, which are crucial for SME sustainability and growth (J. Ha et al., 2022; Q. S. A. Ali et al., 2023). SME owners provided actionable steps for integrating disaster preparedness training and innovative technologies within organizations, including establishing robust data systems, workforce structures, and readiness frameworks to mitigate disruptive events (Seong et al., 2023; T. Oyama et al., 2021). Recommendations for supportive policies addressing financial constraints and providing resources for SMEs were also highlighted (Murray & Rawat, 2021).

From a societal perspective, the study emphasized the importance of disaster preparedness for SMEs, recognizing their significance to the economy. Tennessee was chosen as the focus of this study due to its unique economic landscape and the significant role SMEs play in the state's economy. SMEs constituted 99.9% of private sector organizations and 60% of employers in Tennessee, contributing 47% of business turnover to the state's economy (Coates et al., 2019). Therefore, the study highlighted the need to promote readiness and develop strategies to mitigate the impact of disasters on communities.

For instance, Tennessee experienced several disruptive events, such as the wildfires in Sevier County in 2016, which caused significant economic losses and highlighted the need for improved disaster preparedness integration by SME owners (S. Ha et al., 2022). The state's diverse range of businesses and vulnerability to natural disasters make it an ideal setting to explore how innovative and technology-driven disaster preparedness solutions enhance SME resilience.

By focusing on Tennessee, the study aimed to provide tailored insights and practical solutions that can be applied to SMEs within the state, addressing their specific challenges and contributing to their overall sustainability and growth. Therefore, future research will explore the long-term impacts of the lack of integrated technology-driven disaster preparedness on SME resilience while examining similar strategies in different contexts (Hoerold et al., 2021; L. Karlı et al., 2022).

This exploratory case study presented Tennessee SME owners' need to adopt innovative and technology-driven disaster preparedness solutions that were both protective and sustainable (L. Karlı et al., 2022). Determining solutions was essential for strategically preserving, responding to, and recovering from disruptive events by SME owners and managers (Alexander & Harris, 2020; F. Ali et al., 2023; J. Ha et al., 2022). The study investigation was guided by the COR theoretical framework, qualitative research methodology, and exploratory case study design to understand the need for SME owners to implement technology-driven and innovative disaster preparedness solutions to build organizational resilience.

The economic significance of SMEs in Tennessee cannot be overstated, as small business owners provide employment opportunities, integrate innovative strategies, and contribute to the state's revenue growth. SME owners play a crucial role as economic contributors in various cities across Tennessee, highlighting the importance of implementing technology-driven disaster preparedness solutions to mitigate disaster risks and vulnerabilities (J. Ha et al., 2022). Furthermore, adopting policies and frameworks by SME owners promoted the implementation of technology-driven and innovative disaster preparedness solutions and integration of readiness training, leveraging a resilient business culture, enabling effective response against disruptive events (Q. S. A. Ali et al., 2023; Sarmiento et al., 2019).

Technology-driven disaster preparedness solutions have been crucial for SME owners as they recover from disruptive events (Asgary et al., 2020; Coates et al., 2019; Sarmiento et al., 2019; Utami et al., 2021). One vital resolution SME leaders have prioritized is DRR, which enhances business resilience and establishes a robust framework to withstand disruptive events (Sarmiento et al., 2019).

SME owners, managers, incident response workforce, and stakeholders have been advised to advocate for awareness training, drills, and exercises to empower the workforce, as confirmed during the research study (Sadeghi et al., 2022; T. Oyama et al., 2021; Y. Oyama et al., 2021). Effective BCM plans were identified as essential for minimizing disruptive events' impacts on business operations, as stated among SME owners (Coates et al., 2019).

Some SME owners have improved business resilience against disruptive events by implementing specific policies and frameworks such as BCM, DR, and CP while integrating additional solutions to facilitate risk assessment, mitigation strategies, BC, and DR (Sadeghi et al., 2022). Prioritizing technology-driven and innovative disaster preparedness solutions is crucial for SME owners as it assures BC during unforeseen circumstances (Q. S. A. Ali et al., 2023). In Tennessee, SME owners have recognized the importance of promoting technology-driven disaster preparedness solutions and readiness training to raise awareness within their organizations (F. Ali et al., 2023; T. Oyama et al., 2021).

Small business owners continue to face frequent disruptive events, underscoring the importance of safeguarding infrastructure, critical data, valuable resources, and the workforce (Sarmiento et al., 2019). The importance of implementing disaster preparedness solutions for Tennessee

SME owners to preserve valuable investments from disruptive events is further elaborated in Chapter 2 on the current state of the existing body of knowledge through the Literature Review.

Existing Knowledge and Gaps

The purpose of this exploratory case study was to investigate how Tennessee SME owners should implement innovative and technology-driven disaster preparedness solutions to enhance business resilience and integrate effective resolutions towards disruptive events. The problem discussed in this study involved the challenges faced by Tennessee SME owners in the implementation of innovative and technology-driven disaster preparedness solutions, which often leads to early business closure and negatively impacts the state's economy (J. Ha et al., 2022; Leary et al., 2023; T. Oyama et al., 2021).

Technology-driven disaster preparedness solutions were identified as crucial for preserving valuable resources against disruptive events (J. Ha et al., 2022; Leary et al., 2023; Sarmiento et al., 2019; T. Oyama et al., 2021). In Chapter 2, the research presented an overview of the literature review presenting the need for implementing technology-driven disaster preparedness solutions for SME owners from diverse industries.

Sub-topics discussed in the review of the literature in Chapter 2 are as follows:

(a) Historical background of disaster preparedness,

(b) Challenges hindering disaster preparedness,

(c) Consequences of unpreparedness,

(d) Enforcing innovative preparedness training,

(e) Technologically innovative preparedness solutions,

(f) Innovative preparedness policies and frameworks,

(g) Importance of preparedness.

Case Study Strategies

The overview in the literature indicated that implementing effective technology-driven disaster preparedness solutions by SME owners promotes a resilient readiness posture. This exploratory case study and literature review investigated the implementation of technology-driven disaster preparedness solutions to promote readiness within organizations.

The literature review searches were accomplished using the National University Library online through the Roadrunner advanced search engine for key terms, including *business continuity management, business resilience, cyberattacks, disaster, disaster preparedness, disaster recovery, disaster risk reduction, disruptive events, service-dominant logic, small to medium-sized enterprises,* and *technology-driven disaster preparedness.*

To obtain relevant research findings, search engines used for this study were *Google Scholar, Ulrichsweb, and SpringerLink*; databases entailed *SAGE Journals, Ebook Central, SpringerLink, ProQuest*, and *Wiley Online Library* to find peer-reviewed journal articles and eBooks relevant to the literature. Journal articles also included specific specialty books with definitive topics and keywords. The years for peer-reviewed journal articles ranged from less than one year to 5 years, except for the theoretical framework.

Guiding Theoretical Framework

The guiding theoretical framework for this qualitative exploratory case study was the COR theory created by Professor Stevan E. Hobfoll (Hobfoll, 1989). The COR theory is a framework business owners or individuals follow to identify processes for obtaining, protecting, and preserving invested and valuable resources. Adhering to the COR theory, small business owners considered investments valuable by categorizing resources as gains or losses (Nath et al., 2024).

This study indicated a foundational understanding of the advantages of implementing effective disaster-preparedness solutions for SME owners as they protect valuable assets and differentiate gains from losses (Cai et al., 2023; Hobfoll, 2001; Pradhan et al., 2024). Resource gains were identified as objects promoting business operations, such as equipment, workforce, and revenue increase (Cai et al., 2023). On the contrary, according to the COR theory, resource loss is determined after assessing the remaining assets following a disruptive event, incident intensity, and consequences.

In contrast, COR theory was compared against the Selective Optimization with Compensation (SOC) theory created by Paul Baltes in 1997, whereby the objective presented how valuable resources would be retained or lost upon experiencing a disastrous event (Hobfoll et al., 2018). Baltes and Hobfoll discussed the identification and determination of how to proceed with remaining resources to determine whether both theories consisted of effective methods to compensate for valuable resources lost or remaining assets upon experiencing a disastrous event.

The COR theory has been compared to Baltes's SOC theory, with recommendations to integrate both theories for shared collaborative ideas. Although Hobfoll sought concepts from Baltes to establish the COR theory, Baltes's theory was incompatible with this study, so the COR theoretical framework was chosen for this particular study (Hobfoll et al., 2018). Therefore, the COR theory by Hobfoll focuses on how individuals and organizations strive to acquire, retain, and protect valuable resources, preventing stress and promoting well-being (Hobfoll et al., 2018).

Baltes' SOC theory emphasizes how individuals adapt to age-related changes and losses by selecting and optimizing their resources and compensating for declines. This comparison indicates how valuable resources can be retained or lost upon experiencing a disastrous event. This study is built on the COR theory to present how SME owners in Tennessee implement innovative disaster preparedness solutions to address challenges in preserving valuable resources, integrating effective procedures to overcome barriers, fostering a culture oriented toward technology-driven disaster preparedness, and applying these theoretical principles to enhance resilience.

The integration of COR theory indicates business owners' use of different strategies to protect valuable assets while investing new resources (Alexander & Harris, 2020; Hobfoll, 2001; Pradhan et al., 2024). The new resources are considered critical and valuable by SME owners who acquire them and ensure protection for these new assets is made available. The COR theory selected for this study indicates how SME owners can be guided in protecting valuable resources following effective procedures (Cai et al., 2023).

Moreover, COR theory patterns present how SME owners' resources can be impacted by disastrous events changing over time, whereby it is important to mitigate disaster risks by implementing two basic principles and four corollaries (Hobfoll, 2001). The principles of the COR theory include four corollaries that outline a strategy for creating an environment that preserves and protects valuable resources from disastrous events (Hobfoll et al., 2018). The two basic principles presented how SME owners protected and procured assets identified as beneficial or valuable for business growth (Hobfoll, 2001; Pradhan et al., 2024).

Valuable resource categories indicated how the dependence on groups is set apart as selected essential resources, while correlating to the two fundamental principles of the COR theory. The two principles consist of (a) resource loss, also considered a risk of losing valuable resources and is not equal to resource gain, and (b) business owners often invest in protective measures to preserve valuable resources from loss, recovery processes, or to gain additional resources (Pradhan et al., 2024). These two principles further present four corollaries of the COR theory by identifying efficient methods to protect valuable investments and assets (Hobfoll et al., 2018).

The four essential corollaries of the COR theory created by Hobfoll (2001) entail different strategies: Corollary 1 indicates ownership of less valuable resources leads to fewer remaining resources after experiencing a disastrous event; Corollary 2 presents loss of valuable resources at an early stage affected organizational gains at a later stage; Corollary 3 addresses business resource gains at an early stage leading to an increase in gains at the development stage regardless of a reduction in business growth, thereby avoiding losses at a later stage; and Corollary 4 presenting how business owners strive to protect undestroyed resources to preserve what is left following a disastrous event (Hobfoll, 2001; Pradhan et al., 2024). These four corollaries from the COR theory were designed for business owners, individuals, and communities, as detailed in the following sections.

Corollary 1

The first corollary of COR theory explains how resources, such as assets or investments owned, should be proactively reinvested using small steps to determine lesser access to shared resources (Nath et al., 2024). The inability to invest in future revenue growth through the integration of disaster risk management underscores the importance of implementing such measures proactively before a disastrous event occurs. This first corollary presents the importance of the fewer business owners' resources or assets and how they can be affected by a disruptive event through loss or other factors. Applying technology-driven disaster preparedness solutions following the first corollary will guide SME owners to invest minimal resources, often reducing organizational loss. The first corollary identifies the importance of resource protection procedures, leading to the second corollary.

Corollary 2

The second corollary of the COR theory addresses resource loss during a preliminary phase, leading to resource loss at a later stage (Nath et al., 2024; Pradhan et al., 2024). Equally, the second corollary guides business owners to understand the importance of technology-driven disaster preparedness against uncertainties. The constant resource loss challenges create organizational stress and overall loss outcomes (Hoerold et al., 2021; Pradhan et al., 2024).

For instance, when SME owners lose valuable resources during the beginning phase of business operations through a disastrous event, a subsequent loss is imminent at a later stage. Moreover, SME owners' implementation of technology-driven disaster preparedness solutions mitigates overwhelming losses, whereby fewer reinvestment resources and decreased reserves will be available for future business investments. Therefore, the second corollary guides SME owners in determining what resources are lost and identifying what progressive efforts contribute to reinstating lost resources, thereby introducing the third corollary.

Corollary 3

The third corollary of the COR theory indicates that valuable assets or investments gained at an early stage from pre-existing resources lead to the maximization of organizational value (Nath et al., 2024; Pradhan et al., 2024). Maximizing valuable resources affirmed the elements of the third corollary of gains in an early phase, leading to an increase at a later phase. The third corollary indicates resources are considered gains to support business owners from loss, depending less on excess for survival after experiencing a disruptive event. Business owners benefit from invested future resources as gains following a disruptive event, thereby introducing the fourth corollary.

Corollary 4

The fourth corollary addressed business owners' preservative efforts of the remaining resources following a disastrous event to minimize the loss of all assets (Nath et al., 2024; Pradhan et al., 2024). This motivates SME owners to preserve valuable resources while avoiding additional losses. A protective posture integrated by SME owners should preserve the remaining resources or assets if a loss has been incurred after experiencing a disruptive event. Business owners should focus on preserving and safeguarding remaining valuable assets while evaluating whether resources can be reinvested.

Historical Presentation of the COR Theory

The four COR theory corollaries presented elements SME owners integrated to mitigate effective technology-driven disaster preparedness solutions against disruptive events to ensure critical data and valuable resources are protected and effectively preserved (Alexander & Harris, 2020; Nath et al., 2024). SME owners used strategies presented by the COR theory as guidance to understand the principles of protecting valuable resources from loss or gain while effectively protecting valuable investments and resources against disastrous events (Hobfoll, 2001; Pradhan et al., 2024).

Historically, COR theory has been documented by scholars as a phenomenon with procedures SME owners can integrate to promote readiness and effectively protect valuable assets against disruptive events (Hobfoll, 2001; Pradhan et al., 2024). In addition, COR theory denotes how resources, including assets and investments, will be protected against disastrous events by demonstrating the role of identifying stress results accompanying the loss or gain of resources.

For the past few decades, COR theory signified related attributes in which different SME owners implemented technology-driven disaster preparedness solutions to test business responsiveness using adaptive and effective readiness skills (Hobfoll et al., 2018; Serenko et al., 2024; T. Oyama et al., 2021). As specified in this exploratory case study, COR theory introduces an understanding of SME owners' integration of innovative disaster preparedness training solutions.

Past empirical studies indicated COR theory presented effective disaster preparedness solutions that guided SME owners to preserve and protect valuable resources (C. Wang et al., 2023; Cai et al., 2023; Nath et al., 2024; T. Oyama et al., 2021). Equally, COR theory indicated an approach SME owners would follow to promote an understanding of protecting, gaining, and preserving critical tenets, in addition to integrating strategic policies and frameworks to address environmental and political dynamic changes (Alexander & Harris, 2020; Nath et al., 2024; Pradhan et al., 2024; T. Oyama et al., 2021).

Small business owners adherence to principles and corollaries extracted from the COR theory to implement technologically-driven disaster preparedness solutions as directional tenets for preserving and protecting critical data and valuable resources is vital. Consequently, SME owners understood the purpose of directional principles from the COR theory, preparing organizations against disastrous events as a mitigatory theoretical approach (Hobfoll, 2001, 2018; Nath et al., 2024).

The COR theory outlined a process that began with specific situational circumstances where individuals, such as SME owners, could deploy technology-driven disaster preparedness solutions while establishing procedures to safeguard valuable assets (Nath et al., 2024). Despite the recognition of valuable resource losses or gains as burdens under the COR theory, numerous scholars and business owners have employed this theory for the past 30 years, and it remains widely cited.

Indication of The COR Theory's Relevance to The Study

The relevance of the exploratory case study research highlighted the significance of the COR theory in guiding other studies focused on enhancing readiness performance among the organizational workforce. However, it also showed that such efforts could be challenging if SME owners do not promote technology-driven disaster preparedness training and development (Nath et al., 2024; Serenko et al., 2024; Silva & Pinto, 2024; T. Oyama et al., 2021).

Innovative and technology-driven disaster preparedness training was essential for integrating readiness solutions, from foundational training performance to implementing mitigatory strategies against disastrous events (Hobfoll et al., 2018; Serenko et al., 2024; T. Oyama et al., 2021). The COR theoretical principles present disaster preparedness guidelines for SME owners to effectively implement training and development initiatives for the incident response workforce while motivating and preparing them to adapt to different circumstances through readiness training.

This exploratory case study indicates the advantages of the COR theory for the integration of functional and adaptive components, preventing the loss of valuable assets and ensuring BC persists. These COR theoretical components guided SME owners in developing mitigatory strategies as they strived to protect valuable assets, infrastructure, critical data, and the workforce (Cai et al., 2023; Nath et al., 2024; Serenko et al., 2024; T. Oyama et al., 2021). Workforce readiness training was crucial in minimizing the impact and stress during and after disruptive events (T. Oyama et al., 2021).

Scholars have selected the COR theory for studies to demonstrate an understanding of disastrous events impacts affecting SME owners and their organizations (T. Oyama et al., 2021). The integration of the COR theory from historical to current research has persisted through various empirical studies, consistently reminding SME owners of the disruptive effects of disastrous events on revenue growth and business sustainability (Nath et al., 2024; Pradhan et al., 2024).

Pradhan et al. (2024) elucidated how current studies reference COR theory to build trust in leadership efforts and promote workforce well-being by integrating technology-driven disaster preparedness. Conversely, the COR theory highlighted the importance of implementing disaster preparedness solutions to protect the workforce and business structures, secure critical information, and safeguard valuable resources, all while promoting successful business operations (Hobfoll, 1989).

Integration of the COR Theory

The COR theory established a foundation for SME owners and their workforce by emphasizing the importance of implementing innovative and technology-driven disaster preparedness through the empowerment and enforcement of training initiatives and promoting adequate security within organizations (Cai et al., 2023; Pradhan et al., 2024; T. Oyama et al., 2021).

Conversely, the implementation of disaster preparedness solutions by SME owners, in line with the COR theory, guided the workforce's well-being. Thus, adopting coping readiness mechanisms and skills was essential for developing a solid and robust incident response workforce within the organization (Nath et al., 2024; T. Oyama et al., 2021).

Small business owners integrate technology-driven disaster preparedness solutions to protect, retain, or replace valuable assets following unexpected disruptive events if the disruption originates from the lack of readiness or implementation of protective solutions. The COR theory should be integrated to guide SME owners to preserve, nurture, and safeguard all invested valuable resources (Hobfoll et al., 2018; Nath et al., 2024).

Consequently, the COR theory was integral to SME owners' disaster preparedness processes by promoting coping mechanisms following disruptive events. This was particularly important for preserving employment resources while maintaining monetary income, seniority, and organizational values (Nath et al., 2024). This study advances the COR theory by applying it to disaster preparedness for SME owners, thereby highlighting the practical implications of resource preservation of valuable business resources. This application demonstrates how effectively managing and conserving valuable resources can enhance business resilience and mitigate the adverse impacts of disasters on SMEs.

Modern Approaches and Ideas: A literature Overview

In reviewing the literature on disaster preparedness and resilience among SME owners, several pivotal studies provided valuable insights into the adoption of innovative technology-driven solutions, the development of robust incident response teams, and the implementation of BCM frameworks, whereby key research by Alexander et al. (2023), Asgary et al. (2020), Hobfoll et al. (2018), S. Ha et al. (2022), Shweta et al. (2022), and Q. S. A. Ali et al. (2023) highlighted the critical role of advanced technologies like AI and blockchain in enhancing disaster preparedness.

Additionally, Cai et al. (2023) and Nath et al. (2024) emphasized the importance of comprehensive training programs and continuous improvement processes for organizational resilience. However, gaps remain in practical implementation, financial challenges, long-term sustainability, and the emotional and psychological impacts of disasters on SME owners.

Summary of Literature Key Studies

Table 1. Summary of Literature Key Studies

Author/Year	Key Points in Publication	Gap
Asgary et al. (2020)	• Presented the lack of adaptation plans • SME owners' dependency on external financial resources	• The size of SMEs and their role in the economy relies on integrating risk reduction, whereby additional research is needed to understand various aspects of risk management.
Q. S. A. Ali et al. (2023)	• Integrating BCM practices within SMEs. • Importance of BCM in protecting SMEs from potential disruptions. • BCM practices to manage the crisis by SME owners. • Effectiveness of planned resilience strategies.	• Current literature shows a lack of urgency in framing the BCM framework with organizational resilience, specifically in SME settings. • SME owners can ensure organizations protect themselves from potential risks and ensure continued resilience. • BCM implementations by SME owners and determining valuable steps towards enhancing the chances of integration success.

Author/Year	Key Points in Publication	Gap
S. Ha et al. (2022)	<ul><li>Critical lack of disaster preparedness inhibiting timely business recovery.</li><li>Disasters cause significant damage to SME facilities and infrastructure, including causalities, revenue loss, and damages to business buildings, equipment, and inventory.</li></ul>	<ul><li>Researchers continue to find that SME owners are unprepared for business recovery following a disastrous event.</li><li>The financial circumstances affect the extent to which SME owners adapt to organizational disaster readiness.</li></ul>
Hobfoll et al. (2018)	<ul><li>Emphasized the COR theory in disaster preparedness.</li><li>Provided a theoretical framework for understanding resource management during disasters.</li></ul>	<ul><li>Practical implementation and impact.</li></ul>
Alexander et al. (2023)	<ul><li>Explored the integration of technology in the incident response workforce.</li><li>Presented the benefits of advanced technologies in improving disaster response capabilities.</li></ul>	<ul><li>Long-term sustainability and adaptability.</li></ul>

Author/Year	Key Points in Publication	Gap
Cai et al. (2023)	• Stressed the need for comprehensive training programs. • Emphasized the role of continuous training in building organizational resilience.	• Limited research on the long-term sustainability and adaptability of disaster preparedness initiatives.
Nath et al. (2024)	• Advocated for continuous improvement processes. • Highlighted the importance of feedback mechanisms in refining disaster preparedness strategies.	• Emotional and psychological impact.

Note. Table 1 summarized the key studies and outlines the identified gaps, presenting a foundation for understanding the essential elements and areas of improvement in innovative disaster preparedness solutions that SME owners, managers, and stakeholders should invest in.

When SME owners, managers, and stakeholders invested in technology-driven and innovative disaster preparedness solutions, it facilitated opportunities to protect valuable assets during emergent situations (Nath et al., 2024). By implementing technology-driven disaster preparedness solutions, SME owners will recover financial investments and better understand how to protect valuable assets and resources.

Nath et al. (2024) further elaborated that the COR theory's guidance to SME owners, managers, and stakeholders encourages the adoption of innovative and technology-driven disaster preparedness solutions, which can aid in preserving and protecting valuable resources. COR theory stood out because its principles and corollaries highlighted the importance of preserving valuable investment resources, particularly when evaluated against other theoretical frameworks (Serenko et al., 2024).

The COR theory, developed by Hobfoll (1989), was a key guiding principle in this study, which posits that individuals and organizations strive to obtain, retain, and protect their valuable resources. This theoretical framework informed the interview questions and coding framework by emphasizing the importance of resource management in disaster preparedness. The interview questions were designed to explore how SME owners prioritized and managed resources such as financial assets, technology, and human capital in the context of disaster preparedness.

The coding framework, developed using NVivo software, categorized the data into sub-themes and themes that reflected resource acquisition, preservation, and allocation strategies. This approach ensured a comprehensive analysis of how SMEs can build resilience and mitigate the impacts of disruptive events by effectively managing their resources, aligning with the COR theory's core principles (Hobfoll, 1989).

The COR theoretical framework aligned well with the qualitative exploratory study due to its principles and corollaries. Consequently, the COR theory guided the qualitative exploratory case study by providing solutions to protect business-critical data and valuable resources (Nath et al., 2024; T. Oyama et al., 2021). Therefore, the COR theory and the study aligned with the purpose statement, problem statement, and research questions to explore effective technology-driven disaster preparedness solutions that SME owners should implement to protect valuable resources and investments.

Historical Background of Disaster Preparedness & Understanding of New Technologies

Disastrous events have continued to significantly impact SMEs in the state of Tennessee, severely affecting business continuity due to the destruction of valuable business assets and organizational structures (J. Ha et al., 2022). Historically, SME owners have faced significant challenges due to disasters impacting organizational operations, which often led to the closure of numerous small businesses and, eventually, revenue loss (Hoerold et al., 2021; S. Ha et al., 2022; T. Oyama et al., 2021; Tosun & Bostan, 2021).

Implementing technology-driven disaster preparedness solutions among SME owners in Tennessee has been minimally documented or reported, highlighting a significant research gap in the literature. The Tennessee District Small Business Administration (SBA) provides services and archives information on incidents, funding programs, counseling, and recovery procedures to support SME owners in Tennessee; however, there is a lack of documented integration of technology-driven disaster preparedness (Gwon et al., 2022; Sarmiento et al., 2019; Tennessee, n.d.).

SBA is an institution that supports and defines SMEs as privately owned and operated businesses in diverse industries, such as tourism, automotive, healthcare, education, and hospitality, with minimal capital margins. Bourdin et al. (2024)

highlighted that future research should continue to provide SME owners with the knowledge necessary to develop preparedness solutions. These solutions are essential tools for determining, gathering, and sustaining the preservation of valuable resources.

Sevier County Wildfires

The extent of disaster preparedness investment for the wildfires that occurred between November and December of 2016, which spread over 17,000 acres in Sevier County, Tennessee, needed exploration, according to S. Ha et al. (2022) and Sarmiento et al. (2019). As stated by researchers, the challenges SME owners faced in Sevier County during the fire travesty demonstrated the need for effective technology-driven disaster preparedness solutions to mitigate unexpected disruptive events (S. Ha et al., 2022; Sarmiento et al., 2019).

The Sevier County wildfires impacted numerous SMEs, including 73 commercial properties; thousands of residents were evacuated, lives were lost, and critical data and valuable assets were destroyed. The effect on Sevier County SMEs could have been partially due to the lack of effective technology-driven disaster preparedness solutions, which delayed disaster recovery processing timelines (Gwon et al., 2022; Hoerold et al., 2021; S. Ha et al., 2022). The need for SME owners to invest in technology-driven disaster preparedness solutions is still being explored to determine effective methods to protect valuable assets while minimizing revenue loss and focusing on business objectives (F. Ali et al., 2023; Gwon et al., 2022; J. Ha et al., 2022; Sarmiento et al., 2019; Tennessee, n.d.).

Historical Disaster Preparedness Management

Small business owners' historical lack of implementation and management of technology-driven disaster preparedness led to a reduction in government agencies' provision of disaster recovery support, thereby affecting business continuity (Asgary et al., 2020; J. Ha et al., 2022; Lee & Chen, 2021; Y. Oyama et al., 2021). Alexander and Harris (2020), Ali et al. (2021), Hoerold et al. (2021), Ruiz-Cantisani et al. (2020), Shweta et al. (2022), and Q. S. A. Ali et al. (2023) determined that SMEs' lack of innovative and technology-driven disaster preparedness solutions was due to several factors, including business vulnerabilities.

Business vulnerabilities often encompass minimal financial resources, an untrained incident response workforce, and a lack of readiness frameworks or policies. These issues hindered the strengthening of organizational resilience through mitigatory strategies and the improvement of business maturity status (Alexander & Harris, 2020; Ali et al., 2021; Hoerold et al., 2021; Q. S. A. Ali et al., 2023; Ruiz-Cantisani et al., 2020; Shweta et al., 2022).

The lack of technology-driven disaster preparedness implementation by SME owners has continued to be reported until disaster strikes, leading to financial loss, an existential factor often leading to early business closure. Historical reports from scholars, researchers, and business owners have documented SME owners' unidentified risks and vulnerabilities within organizations, which have continued to impact business operations negatively (Alexander & Harris, 2020; Ali et al., 2021; F. Ali et al., 2023; Hoerold et al., 2021; Ruiz-Cantisani et al., 2020; Shweta et al., 2022). Unidentified risks and vulnerabilities emerging among SMEs should have been monitored and mitigated to determine effective vulnerability mitigation strategies (VMSs) for business operations to continue with uninterrupted organizational performance.

Business performance was improved by integrating VMSs, which were incorporated as part of a contingency plan to strengthen SMEs through practical operational abilities (Ali et al., 2021; Shweta et al., 2022). Integrating a contingency plan by SME owners helps mitigate challenging factors, such as disastrous outcomes, to avoid business closure following a disruptive event through recovery strategies, which include visibility, flexibility, and revenue growth. Visibility strategies introduce transparency and financial strength for all firm transactions, supporting SME owners by enhancing operational abilities and business goals to maximize revenue growth. Some vulnerabilities that SME owners continue to be challenged by affect organizational performance if not mitigated promptly.

One significant challenge SME owners faced was financial limitations due to high-interest loans from banks to restore damaged resources, such as transportation, healthcare shortages, human resource loss, and unavailability of services (Ali et al., 2021; Shweta et al., 2022). The need for additional financial resources for SME owners to implement disaster preparedness was a deficit in maintaining daily operations, ultimately affecting business growth and the innovative, technology-driven, evolving economy. SME owners often decline such loans due to elevated risk margins and complicated procedures, thereby minimizing their ability to invest in organizational disaster preparedness. Financial limitations that SME owners face have been increasingly rising, which hinders small business owners from securing bank loan approvals without collateral, thereby leading to overall risk maximization.

Challenges Hindering Disaster Preparedness

SMEs are a major driver of economic growth in Tennessee, contributing 90% of revenue and providing over 50% of employment opportunities; however, SME owners continue to face challenges that remain unaddressed due to limited resources (Asgary et al., 2020; Eggers, 2020; J. Ha et al., 2022; Mishra et al., 2023; Q. S. A. Ali et al., 2023). SME owners faced uncontrollable challenges while mitigating disastrous events. Some obstacles they were challenged by included elevated costs, constrained regulations, and an increase in emerging competitors (Asgary et al., 2020; J. Ha et al., 2022; Mishra et al., 2023; Q. S. A. Ali et al., 2023; Ruiz-Cantisani et al., 2020; Tosun & Bostan, 2021).

Mishra et al. (2023) confirmed the importance of mitigating risks affecting SMEs' evolving markets, such as the automotive industry, which was considered a revenue generator and high contributor to the state's economy and was crucial.

Similarly, SME owners faced challenges in meeting the demands of consumers and regulators, which were primarily prevalent among small businesses (Gwon et al., 2022; Lee & Chen, 2021; Tosun & Bostan, 2021; Y. Oyama et al., 2021).

Some challenges that SME owners faced included: (a) Lack of financial resources to sustain supply chain initiatives, (b) Lack of or limited visibility and resources for best practices, such as a trained workforce to initiate and implement sustainable technology-driven mitigatory strategies (c) Outstanding regulatory procedures and maintenance (d) Lack of innovative or modern technology, such as disaster preparedness software tools. The lack of financial resources posed obstacles that hindered SME owners from integrating efficient policies and technology-driven disaster preparedness solutions (Sarmiento et al., 2019; Varga-Florez et al., 2020).

Outcomes of Challenging Factors

Challenges faced by SME owners can be deterring due to the lack of revenue growth and consistent strategic approach to match competitive markets (Gwon et al., 2022; Lee & Chen, 2021; T. Oyama et al., 2021; Tosun & Bostan, 2021). In addition, SME owners' lack of innovative disaster risk management integration introduces evolving challenges through (a) lack of resources to preserve valuable assets requiring adequate protection; (b) rescuing the workforce, valuable assets, and infrastructure maintenance following a disruptive event; (c) lack of resources to prepare for pre-disaster or post-disaster impacts against disruptive event; (d) unrenovated locations are vulnerable to the risk of losing invested assets; (e) lack of innovative and technology-driven disaster preparedness training including emergency disaster preparedness and incident response plans; (f) vulnerabilities from risks of break-ins to steal valuable assets and cybercrime; (g) lack of defined incident response workforce leading to post-disastrous financial loss; and (f) failure of government agencies to include SMEs in disaster preparedness initiatives.

Moreover, challenging factors affecting business growth included the lack of workforce readiness originating from (a) lack of technology-driven disaster preparedness training programs, (b) lack of innovative constraints, (c) lack of financial resources to mitigate existing disaster risks, (d) lack of technology-driven disaster preparedness strategies, € economic and legal issues, (f) political attacks, and (g) lack of business recovery procedures (Asgary et al., 2020; J. Ha et al., 2022; Lee & Chen, 2021; Mishra et al., 2023; Tosun & Bostan, 2021).

Asgary et al. (2020), J. Ha et al. (2022), Lee and Chen (2021), Mishra et al. (2023), and Tosun and Bostan (2021) concluded that SME owners need additional resources from government agencies to maximize business resilience.

In addition, raw materials are necessary for SME owners when implementing technology-driven disaster preparedness solutions, which can be challenging, although these readiness resources require coordination at the government level (Alexander & Harris, 2020; Asgary et al., 2020; Hoerold et al., 2021; Lee & Chen, 2021; Ruiz-Cantisani et al., 2020; Tosun & Bostan, 2021). Extreme disastrous events affect SME owners by causing destruction, whereby business operations and BC are disrupted due to the lack of technology-driven disaster preparedness solutions and unmitigated disaster risks and vulnerabilities.

Consequences Of Unpreparedness

Implementing technology-driven disaster preparedness solutions by SME owners should include promoting readiness knowledge against disruptive events, which continues to be researched (Andrade et al., 2022; Mishra et al., 2023; Sarmiento et al., 2019). Following a disastrous event reminds

SME owners of the importance of implementing technology-driven disaster preparedness solutions. Some of the United States' historically devastating disastrous events include "Hurricanes Charley, Frances, Ivan, and Jeanne in 2004; Katrina in 2005; Sandy in 2012; Irma, Maria, and Harvey in 2017; the COVID-19 pandemic in 2020; and the Texas winter storm in 2021" (NIST, 2021; NOAA, 2022). These events caused widespread destruction, loss of infrastructure and employment, structural damage, and increased risks of injury, illnesses, and non-communicable diseases.

Leaving destruction, loss of infrastructure and employment, structural damage, risks of injury, illnesses, and "non-communicable diseases (NCDs; Asgary et al., 2020, p. 2; Hoerold et al., 2021; Leary et al., 2023; S. Ha et al., 2022; Y. Oyama et al., 2021). However, SME owners continue being challenged by the lack of financial resources and efficient policies, which pose obstacles to investing in effective technology-driven disaster preparedness solutions (Sarmiento et al., 2019; Varga-Florez et al., 2020).

Disastrous Experiences

Consequently, disastrous impacts such as NCDs were identified by SME owners as important in implementing innovative and technology-driven disaster preparedness training initiatives. Other disastrous consequences affecting SME infrastructures include communication flow disruptions, lack of medical services, and loss of employment, further affecting BC (Asgary et al., 2020; Green, 2023; Gwon et al., 2022; Leary et al., 2023; Saad et al., 2021; Sarmiento et al., 2019). SME owners continue facing challenges from disastrous event impacts, also known as disaster experiences (DE); for instance, power and water outages, supply chain disruptions, machinery structure destruction, loss of inventory, and communication disruptions.

Additionally, unidentified risks and vulnerabilities continue to affect SME productivity due to the lack of technology-driven disaster preparedness implementation. Mitigating risks and vulnerabilities should be manageable for SME owners, managers, and the incident response workforce to ensure their main objective focuses on the upkeep of technologically innovative disaster preparedness solutions to preserve valuable resources (Asgary et al., 2020; Q. S. A. Ali et al., 2023).

The combination of disastrous events and the absence of technology-driven disaster preparedness solutions frequently delayed and complicated business recovery efforts, as assets, critical data, and workforce displacement became significant challenges (Alexander & Harris, 2020; Asgary et al., 2020; J. Ha et al., 2022; Leary et al., 2023; Sarmiento et al., 2019; T. Oyama et al., 2021). The severity of the impacts of disastrous events highlighted the need for SME owners to adopt technologically innovative disaster readiness solutions while enhancing organizational resilience. The long-term disadvantages of these post-disaster events often made it challenging for SMEs to return to their previous state, thereby affecting the continuity of business operations and the overall state economy.

Alexander and Harris (2020), Asgary et al. (2020), J. Ha et al. (2022), Leary et al. (2023), Sarmiento et al. (2019), and T. Oyama et al. (2021) investigated the impacts of disastrous events on SME owners, finding that such events often resulted in business closures and workforce displacement. The loss of employment due to disastrous events introduced post-traumatic stress disorder (PTSD), leading to health issues that often resulted in self-harm stemming from loss of hope and devastation (Alexander & Harris, 2020).

Technologically Innovative Disaster Preparedness Solutions

Emerging technologies and innovative disaster preparedness solutions promoted SMEs' organizational resilience to maximize revenue growth and the overall state's economy (Asgary et al., 2020; Q. S. A. Ali et al., 2023). Disaster preparedness implementation by SME owners using innovative and trending technology such as artificial intelligence (AI) driven tools, data backup processes, cloud computing, smartphones, robotics, and drones, promoting readiness solutions.

Automating trending and innovative technologies by SME owners will enhance work environments to enhance business readiness instead of outsourcing resource protection. Innovative disaster preparedness solutions maximize economic growth by improving business resilience for a stable pre- and post-disaster SME environment. SME owners' initiatives included implementing technology-driven disaster preparedness and innovative solutions, and adequately mitigating risks and vulnerabilities using risk management controls (Asgary et al., 2020; Q. S. A. Ali et al., 2023).

A robust posture is developed if SME owners integrate a resilient foundation with innovative technology-driven disaster preparedness solutions, generating revenue and boosting the economy. Innovative disaster preparedness implementation guided SME owners' decision-making while saving costs (Asgary et al., 2020; Ruiz-Cantisani et al., 2020). SME owners' implementation of technology-driven disaster preparedness solutions progressively enhanced when BCM integrated cyberspace and reliable networking communications (Asgary et al., 2020; Green, 2023; Ruiz-Cantisani et al., 2020).

Understanding the importance of innovative and technology-driven disaster preparedness and implementing solutions demonstrated how SME owners equipped the workforce for pre- and post-disaster events, whereby businesses increased their positive business performance (Eggers, 2020; Ruiz-Cantisani et al., 2020). Innovative solutions incorporated with mitigatory strategies will enable SME owners to integrate acceptable risk management into their organizations while effectively offering monitoring procedures that these organizations can implement.

Establishing a resilient foundation of technology-driven disaster preparedness solutions will motivate SME owners to generate revenue and boost the economy. Integrating disaster preparedness with innovative ideas guided decision-making outcomes while saving costs (Asgary et al., 2020; Green, 2023; Ruiz-Cantisani et al., 2020). Understanding these solutions helped SME owners prepare for pre- and post-disastrous events, promoting business growth and positive performance outcomes (Eggers, 2020; Ruiz-Cantisani et al., 2020).

In addition, innovative solutions indicated tolerable risks and effective continuous monitoring procedures. Innovative disaster preparedness solutions implemented by SME owners will enhance readiness skills; however, they also considered that disruptive events could include emerging technology-initiated challenges affecting business operations, which could undermine organizational resilience (Ruiz-Cantisani et al., 2020).

Emerging technology-initiated disruptive events included (a) Data and communication technology bottleneck, (b) Unimproved disaster preparedness training resources for the incident response workforce, (c) Lack of improved value in technological systems, (d) Outdated innovative systems, and (e) Elevated levels of unofficial procedures, which often lead to premature SMEs' business closure (Eggers, 2020; Green, 2023; Gwon et al., 2022; Ruiz-Cantisani et al., 2020; T. Oyama et al., 2021). SME owners should explore opportunities for integrating innovative disaster preparedness solutions by addressing definitive and progressive patterns using resilience models to assess the level of readiness solutions comparable to actual business equity.

Maturity Model Exploration

Technologically innovative tools to mitigate risks and vulnerabilities were identified by SME owners and the incident response workforce while determining accurate and effective disaster preparedness solutions (Ali et al., 2021; Shweta et al., 2022). Ali et al. (2021) and Shweta et al. (2022) examined the importance of implementing technology-driven and resilient maturity models to sustain organizations from disaster risk affecting SME owners' business growth. For instance, AI and blockchain forecasting tools were identified as feasible due to their consistency in readiness monitoring and data aggregation accuracy by the incident response workforce in times of uncertainty (Ali et al., 2021; Shweta et al., 2022).

However, data collected from continuous monitoring must be scrutinized, especially if the data reported is inaccurate, to help avoid designating incorrect mitigation strategies that could interfere with SME owners' implementation of technology-driven disaster preparedness solutions to preserve resource investments. Consequently, this study encouraged SME owners to adopt technology-driven disaster preparedness solutions to protect the workforce from disruptive events. It is recommended that trauma-informed positive education (TIPE) models be adopted to introduce knowledge interventions and educate vulnerable employees (Alexander & Harris, 2020). SME owners' efforts to implement readiness frameworks and policies inspired the workforce during pre- and post-disaster situations, playing a key role in disaster recovery efforts after a disruptive event.

Innovative Preparedness Policies and Frameworks

The innovative disaster preparedness solutions explored identified the frameworks and policies that SME owners should implement, helping them cultivate a positive response to disruptive events (Alexander & Harris, 2020; Asgary et al., 2020; Green, 2023; Leary et al., 2023; Q. S. A. Ali et al., 2023; Ruiz-Cantisani et al., 2020). Green (2023) and Q. S. A. Ali et al. (2023) encouraged the continuation of future studies to explore effective technology-driven disaster preparedness solutions in terms of implementing frameworks and policies while understanding the importance of readiness integration for strengthening business resilience.

The integration of BCM frameworks and essential disaster preparedness policies by SME owners was found to be hindered by a lack of financial resources, as well as other factors, limiting their ability to explore efficient and affordable solutions suitable for businesses of all sizes (Alexander & Harris, 2020; Asgary et al., 2020; Green, 2023; Leary et al., 2023; Q. S. A. Ali et al., 2023; Ruiz-Cantisani et al., 2020). Small business owners confirmed that frameworks such as BCM and DRR were essential for reducing the impact of disruptive events and ensuring swift integration of disaster recovery procedures (Sarmiento et al., 2019).

Business performance and disaster preparedness capabilities will likely improve if SME owners integrate BCM frameworks and relevant policies, enabling them to withstand disruptive events better and accelerate disaster recovery procedures. BCM frameworks offer effective data-sharing and communication strategies following a disaster, helping to define disaster recovery procedures and implement efficient business continuity operations. A practical BCM framework includes policies and strategies that support essential business operations, mitigate risks, and offer guidance during unforeseen disaster circumstances.

Organizational resilience, built by SME owners by implementing various frameworks, policies, and platforms, is crucial for ensuring reliable supplier dependence (Green, 2023;

Shweta et al., 2022). Green (2023) and Shweta et al. (2022) highlighted that supplier relations management (SRM) is an additional framework SME owners should adopt to stay proactive in monitoring supply chain operations during disruptive events. SRM best practices indicated that guided procedures SME owners followed determined a well-defined communication and collaborative approach to maximize performance and mitigate supply chain risks (Green, 2023; Shweta et al., 2022).

SME owners should weigh in on selected suppliers to ensure they possess minimal financial discrepancies, promptly deliver orders, and maintain a reputable posture. Data transfer between SME owners and suppliers is essential while adhering to secure procedures after establishing a reliable business relationship for sending and receiving critical data. SME owners' integration of risk management procedures reduces financial loss, meets supplier expectations, and improves business performance.

After identifying reliable data communication tools, SME owners ensured secure information sharing with suppliers through Electronic Data Interchange (EDI), APIs, cloud-based collaboration tools, Secure File Transfer Protocol (SFTP), and web-based portals, promoting efficient and secure data transfer (Green, 2023; Shweta et al., 2022). Suppliers establish clear practices for critical information, data sharing, ownership protection, and secure communication by following secure protocol solutions and well-defined standards.

Secure communication protocols offer structured procedures to prevent data loss from small businesses by enhancing training efforts and optimizing supply chain operations, thereby strengthening business resilience in the face of disruptive events. To enhance organizational resilience, SME owners considered integrating BIA with BCM framework practices as a disaster preparedness strategy (Green, 2023; Gwon et al., 2022; T. Oyama et al., 2021).

Business performance improves if SME owners integrate BCM practices to guide prompt responses during or following disastrous events. Then again, F. Ali et al. (2023) confirmed that many SME owners tend to close their businesses after a disaster, primarily due to the failure to implement BCM frameworks, resulting in ineffective recovery procedures and a lack of resilience.

Key priorities in BCM practices included strong leadership, workforce competency, resilience, and the availability of emerging technological systems for operations (Q. S. A. Ali et al., 2023). Therefore, by integrating BCM and government-provided frameworks, SME owners help guide their organizations' business resilience and growth while continuing to emphasize the importance of adopting innovative, technology-driven disaster preparedness solutions to meet readiness expectations.

Government Agencies' Initiated Frameworks

Mitigation strategies implemented by SME owners to build a resilient organizational structure included the adoption of innovative disaster preparedness frameworks provided by government agencies, such as FEMA. Resources like the Rainy Day Fund (RDF) and the Disaster Preparedness Guide (DPG; J. Ha et al., 2022; Lee & Chen, 2021; Sarmiento et al., 2019) have been instrumental. SME owners are encouraged to utilize these resources to mitigate disaster vulnerability risks within their organizations. By incorporating technology-driven disaster preparedness solutions and leveraging FEMA's National Disaster Recovery Framework (NDRF), SME owners enhanced business resilience, reduced vulnerabilities, and accelerated recovery efforts (J. Ha et al., 2022; Lee & Chen, 2021).

Frameworks developed by FEMA have continued to comprehensively cover disaster management areas, including prevention, protection, mitigation, response, and recovery (FEMA, 2023). For instance, the National Prevention Framework includes campaigns like "See Something, Say Something," which promotes public vigilance to prevent threats. The National Protection Framework ensures infrastructure security, as seen in efforts to protect the power grid from cyberattacks.

The National Mitigation Framework focuses on reducing disaster impacts, exemplified by the Fort Myers Hospital Restoration Project post-Hurricane Irma, which included drainage systems and floodproofing. The National Response Framework coordinates disaster response, illustrated by resource deployment during Hurricane Katrina. Lastly, the National Disaster Recovery Framework aids community rebuilding, demonstrated by the post-Superstorm Sandy collaboration to restore infrastructure and housing.

Additionally, incorporating an agent-based simulation framework with the NDRF enhanced disaster preparedness and response efforts (Chen et al., 2023). Some SME owners adhere to the U.S. government emergency management system frameworks, while others do not. J. Ha et al. (2022), Lee and Chen (2021), and Sarmiento et al. (2019) concurred that SME owners adopted an additional bottom-up approach, as outlined in the RDF framework, to better prepare for future disruptive events.

Numerous SME owners and managers who prepared and incorporated the RDF framework within their organizations significantly minimized financial stress and avoided early business closure or employment loss following a disastrous event (J. Ha et al., 2022; Lee & Chen, 2021; Sarmiento et al., 2019). Government agencies' awareness of policy changes guides SME owners in future operations and preparedness.

This includes budgeting for innovative and technology-driven disaster preparedness solutions while increasing reserves to match inflation and mitigate disaster impacts.

Disaster Preparedness Training Initiatives

Effective technology-driven disaster preparedness solutions integrated by committed leadership should determine the importance of an efficiently trained preparedness strategic initiative (Alexander et al., 2023; Leary et al., 2023; Shweta et al., 2022; T. Oyama et al., 2021). SME owners invest in disaster readiness and enhance business resilience by developing a dedicated incident response team of professionals. Additionally, a professional incident response team ensures that consistent and robust disaster preparedness skills are demonstrated during training, mitigating disruptive events and ensuring the stability and resilience of business operations in the face of destruction.

As SME owners and the incident response workforce adhered to consistent training initiatives aligned with constantly evolving disastrous events and embraced a sense of service at any time, integrating technologically innovative business resilience programs became the primary focus (Alexander et al., 2023; Gwon et al., 2022; J. Ha et al., 2022; Leary et al., 2023; Sarmiento et al., 2019; Shweta et al., 2022; T. Oyama et al., 2021). Resilient programs included frameworks and policies that minimized extreme loss, business closure, and community disruption (Alexander et al., 2023; Gwon et al., 2022; Hoerold et al., 2021; Leary et al., 2023; Sarmiento et al., 2019; Shweta et al., 2022; T. Oyama et al., 2021).

The lack of SME owners investing in technology-driven and innovatively disaster preparedness-oriented training and vigilance introduces risks and vulnerabilities accumulating over time, hindering BC following a disastrous event. For instance, pandemics, supply chain disruptions, rising inflation, inaccurate risk assessments, and other disruptive events drive the need for innovative and technology-driven disaster preparedness training, thereby enhancing business stability and resilience. SME owners and the incident response workforce also establish a stable environment by assessing organizational risks and vulnerabilities. They manage disaster risks and contingency planning by adapting to disaster preparedness for unexpected disruptive events.

Enforcing Innovative Preparedness Training

Technology-driven disaster preparedness training was recognized as a crucial initiative for SME owners to maximize revenue growth, primarily contributing to overall GDP and ensuring safe employment environments (F. Ali et al., 2023; Gwon et al., 2022; T. Oyama et al., 2021). SME owners should perform a business impact analysis (BIA) to establish effective and innovative readiness training. This analysis evaluates disaster preparedness, incident response resources, business continuity management (BCM), disaster recovery (DR), contingency planning (CP), training opportunities, and the organization's knowledge posture.

BIA should also assess organizational posture through essential procedures to identify and prioritize strategies implemented by SME owners and the incident response workforce for effective technology-driven disaster preparedness solutions. The BIA framework encompasses evaluating business risks, disruptive outcomes, disaster recovery (DR), incident response plans, tabletop exercises, effective communication, and readiness training (Green, 2023; Gwon et al., 2022; T. Oyama et al., 2021). Therefore, adopting BIA and other frameworks will prioritize enhancing business resilience, reputation, and revenue growth.

Innovative and technology-focused disaster preparedness training was identified as a crucial initiative for SME owners while aiming to integrate readiness knowledge and promote a robust response plan for the incident response workforce, ensuring long-lasting outcomes (Alexander et al., 2023; Green, 2023; Leary et al., 2023; Shweta et al., 2022; T. Oyama et al., 2021). The hierarchical procedures outlined steps to follow developed through mandatory disaster preparedness educational modules and other methods, which initiated an understanding of the dynamics and effects of disasters (Alexander et al., 2023; Green, 2023; Leary et al., 2023; Shweta et al., 2022; T. Oyama et al., 2021).

An established incident response workforce evaluates imminent disastrous events within an organization's surroundings. This effort enabled the team to develop an incident response plan to follow during a disruptive event and enforce post-recovery planning and efforts (Alexander et al., 2023; Green, 2023). Alexander et al. (2023), Green (2023), Leary et al. (2023), Shweta et al. (2022), and T. Oyama et al. (2021) concluded that technology-driven training strategies enforced by SME owners using top-down hierarchical procedures often strengthen the incident response team. Alexander et al. (2023) and Green (2023) introduced radical disaster interpretation (Radix), a collaborative group of scholars and business owners operating for the past two decades to determine the root cause of disastrous events.

Additionally, Radix was recognized as a platform that represented disasters through simulations and documentation of lessons learned from previous disruptive events, identifying remediation strategies preventing disasters from the bottom up and top down in the leadership hierarchy (Alexander et al., 2023; Lee & Chen, 2021). Radix platform points towards strategic directions for distributing responsibilities to business owners and the incident response workforce, using a defined approach to determine measures for preparing against disastrous circumstances, potentially requiring government support.

As a result, Radix operated as a platform with confidence, outlining procedures to improve influential decision-making contributions for disaster-oriented scholars and professionals, connecting and maximizing risk assessments (Alexander et al., 2023; Lee & Chen, 2021). By boosting the confidence of scholars, professionals, and SME owners, the Radix platform facilitated disaster risk reduction and sharing ideas about ongoing events, offering educational benefits, particularly in communication and engagement for disaster recovery (DR). SME owners considered mitigating disastrous events by integrating the contributions explored and supplemented to platforms like Radix.

Business Owners' Investment in Disaster Preparedness

Integrated disaster risk reduction (DRR) strategies to maximize revenue growth focused on the economic roles of stakeholders, while SME owners supported innovative ideas and resource re-utilization (Sarmiento et al., 2019). Sarmiento et al. (2019) examined the effectiveness of business leadership, its importance to SME owners, and organizational economic growth while increasing revenue and overall GDP through employment opportunities. SME owners considered integrating DRR, BCM, RDF, Radix, and SRM frameworks, in addition to updating policies to build organizational resilience and protect business investments and valuable resources (Ali et al., 2021; Sarmiento et al., 2019; Shweta et al., 2022; T. Oyama et al., 2021).

As a result, SME owners' investment in technology-driven disaster preparedness training processes emphasized the importance of preserving valuable resources, achieving revenue growth, maintaining readiness oversight, and implementing risk mitigation strategies. The adoption of DRR and BCM frameworks by SME owners mitigated the effects of disastrous risks by minimizing revenue loss, preserving essential assets, and expediting disaster recovery processes (Ali et al., 2021; Sarmiento et al., 2019; Shweta et al., 2022; T. Oyama et al., 2021).

Incorporating the DRR Index (DRRI) influences business owners by modifying risk metrics to establish mitigatory procedures and cover estimated damage and financial loss resulting from disruptive events, making contingency planning essential. Ali et al. (2021) and Shweta et al. (2022) concluded that SME owners' investment in contingency planning improved trauma intervention during the implementation of technology-driven disaster preparedness solutions.

Frameworks and policy integration by SME owners determined essential initiatives to strengthen organizational resilience through mitigatory strategies and resources (Ali et al., 2021; Sarmiento et al., 2019; Shweta et al., 2022; T. Oyama et al., 2021). To initiate a resilient, sustainable, and secure supply chain environment, SME owners considered implementing an additional framework—a technology-driven disaster preparedness hybrid solution (Ali et al., 2021; Shweta et al., 2022). Ali et al. (2021) and Shweta et al. (2022) highlighted that the integration of a robust hybrid framework prepared SME owners and reassured the workforce and clients during disastrous events by demonstrating established mitigation strategies through business continuity (BC) planning, agility, and adaptability.

The importance of implementing technology-driven disaster preparedness and risk management frameworks to respond to outcomes caused by disruptive events was internationally emphasized by recognized institutions (Hoerold et al., 2021; Tosun & Bostan, 2021; Y. Oyama et al., 2021). The United Nations Educational, Scientific and Cultural Organization (UNESCO); the International Center for the Study of the Preservation and Restoration of Cultural Property (ICCROM); and the International Council of Museums (ICOM) are among the internationally recognized institutions that emphasize the importance of implementing technology-driven disaster preparedness and risk management frameworks to respond to disruptive events, reminding SME owners to protect valuable resources and investments.

Importance of Technology-Driven Disaster Preparedness

Small business owners are encouraged to adopt technology-driven disaster preparedness solutions to protect their business investments, valuable assets, and critical data. Global Risk highlighted the importance of SME owners implementing technology-driven disaster preparedness solutions to establish readiness plans against disruptive events, data breaches by cyber attackers, infectious diseases, and life crises reported by the World Economic Forum (WEF, Asgary et al., 2020; Gwon et al., 2022; T. Oyama et al., 2021). Leary et al. (2023), T. Oyama et al. (2021), and Tosun and Bostan (2021) concluded that SME owners' businesses were highly vulnerable due to low investment portfolios, weak business structures, inadequate contingency planning resources, and a lack of a skilled incident response workforce.

When SME owners comprehended the readiness benefits for their organization and leveraged big data analytics for efficiency, they successfully integrated technology-driven disaster preparedness solutions (Bourdin et al., 2024; Hsu & Sharma, 2023). Significant data benefits referenced SMEs consistently tracked disruptive events while saving lives to minimize destruction with emergency-employed recovery procedures. The lack of a professional workforce adopting ML was emphasized by Bourdin et al. (2024) as a barrier to implementing innovative disaster preparedness solutions in various organizations.

Due to detection capabilities, which rescued the workforce before disastrous outcomes, SME owners implemented Machine/Deep Learning (M/D/L) preparedness tools to preserve valuable resources. Additionally, SME owners contemplated integrating AI-driven tools as disaster preparedness solutions evolved. Consequently, a deep learning framework was considered a crucial resource SME owners implemented to obtain information from social media resources for rescue teams' ability to connect communities while identifying the missing workforce (Hsu & Sharma, 2023). M/D/L and AI tools are essential technology-driven resources that can automatically detect information during crises, assisting the incident response workforce and emergency responders, especially when rescuing employees.

Big data analytics play a crucial role in technology-driven disaster preparedness by continuously monitoring weather calamities, identifying mitigating factors in relief efforts, promoting DR, and reevaluating procedures. Insufficient technological resources among SME owners often result in early business closures following disastrous events. This underscored the need to introduce technology-driven disaster preparedness solutions through training initiatives aimed at cultivating an informed incident response workforce (Hsu & Sharma, 2023; Leary et al., 2023; T. Oyama et al., 2021; Tosun & Bostan, 2021). For instance, SME owners recognize innovative and technology-driven disaster preparedness in healthcare environments, where healthcare professionals receive education to understand the criticality of responding promptly during disruptive events.

Ensuring the continuity of patient care support is essential, and healthcare providers are advised to continuously monitor their environments with vigilance, especially during care delivery. This is particularly important during disasters involving infrastructure damage, power and water shortages, communication constraints, and structural integrity issues. Recording previous experiences as lessons learned in DR was beneficial for sharing knowledge with the incident response team and other staff members, particularly for conducting proactive tabletop exercises and reevaluating existing technology-driven disaster preparedness solutions for enhancement (Leary et al., 2023; T. Oyama et al., 2021; Tosun & Bostan, 2021).

SME owners' prioritization of integrating technology-driven disaster preparedness solutions into training and knowledge-building sessions fosters innovative strategies for post-disaster recovery procedures. SME owners' investment in advanced communication networks, such as global positioning systems, is essential for rescue operations and safeguarding valuable resources (Hsu & Sharma, 2023). Although often overlooked, big data analytics offers indispensable relief for technology-driven disaster preparedness by facilitating risk management during times of crisis.

Workforce Disaster Preparedness

Implementing technology-driven disaster preparedness solutions enhances SME workforce readiness, strengthens business resilience, and enables adaptation to unforeseen challenges like unemployment and poverty. This resilient environment empowered SME owners and their incident response teams to smoothly transition and sustain business operations in the aftermath of a disaster (Gwon et al., 2022; Leary et al., 2023; Saad et al., 2021; T. Oyama et al., 2021; Tosun & Bostan, 2021). Small business owners emphasize the importance of integrating disaster preparedness training and advocating for creating incident response teams.

Thereby maximizing readiness knowledge and ensuring the team understands the benefits of a resilient posture, especially if they have not experienced a disaster. An openly reliable communicative platform established between SME owners and suppliers relies on supply chain best practices. Ali et al. (2021), Green (2023), and Shweta et al. (2022) investigated and promoted a collaborative environment among SME owners and suppliers to securely preserve critical data, considering supplier selection. Credibility verification and expedited delivery should be integrated with efficient communication to ensure adherence to organizational reputation standards.

SME owners understood the importance of integrating efficient communication with suppliers for secure data exchange, which indicated how data was kept confidential and delivered promptly to meet expected outcomes (Ali et al., 2021; Green, 2023; Hsu & Sharma, 2023; Shweta et al., 2022). Developing a robust technology-driven disaster preparedness plan begins with identifying vulnerabilities and risks. Subsequent mitigation strategies were crafted, and a disaster preparedness risk management plan was developed to address and remedy potential issues (Ali et al., 2021; Gwon et al., 2022; Shweta et al., 2022; T. Oyama et al., 2021; Tosun & Bostan, 2021).

SME owners develop and integrate training procedures, safety protocols, and incident response teams to effectively streamline disaster preparedness. They create a coherent risk management plan that outlines guidance for handling disruptive events. Ali et al. (2021), Gwon et al. (2022), Shweta et al. (2022), T. Oyama et al. (2021), and Tosun and Bostan (2021) concluded that a disaster risk management plan was simplified for SME owners, stakeholders, and the incident response workforce to facilitate easy comprehension.

The plan includes (a) an efficient evacuation plan for the workforce during times of disaster, (b) an evaluated state of emergency, (c) a disaster power and communication outage impact level with an alternative plan, (d) tested tabletop exercises, (e) a designated incident response team, (f) technology-driven preparedness training modules, and (g) an innovative disaster recovery (DR) plan of action. Preparedness for SME owners during times of uncertainty involves a well-developed and integrated disaster risk mitigation management plan, which is essential.

Risks and Vulnerabilities Mitigation Strategies

Through effective disaster preparedness by small business owners for unpredictable circumstances, SME owners' implementation of risk mitigation strategies cultivated a resilient organizational setting (Ali et al., 2021; Shweta et al., 2022). The formulated risk mitigation strategies must outline comprehensive and efficient protocols that SME owners can incorporate to proactively address identified risks and vulnerabilities before the onset of disruptive events. Ali et al. (2021) and Shweta et al. (2022) confirmed that mitigating risks or adopting effective strategies is necessary to lessen the loss of businesses and valuable assets affecting SME owners.

SME owners enhance organizational resilience by integrating risk mitigation strategies and facilitating streamlined disaster recovery processes when faced with disruptive events. In addition, expedited and efficient disaster recovery solutions improved business resilience and were achieved through risk and vulnerability mitigation (Ali et al., 2021; Shweta 2022). Business resilience is strengthened by the SMEs' incident response workforce integrating disaster preparedness capabilities to act with immediate readiness towards disruptions.

When SME owners adopted technology-driven disaster preparedness solutions using effective risk and vulnerability mitigation strategies, business resilience was initiated, making it a practical component of revenue growth (Ali et al., 2021; Shweta et al., 2022). Proactive risk mitigation following determined strategies demonstrates how SME owners can face disruptive events in uncertain times through effective disaster preparedness, particularly for unpredictable and unexpected risks. Promoting business growth and stability, SME owners identify and implement strategies to mitigate risks and vulnerabilities within the organization, documenting crucial steps and lessons learned.

As SME owners aimed to mitigate organizational risks and vulnerabilities, policymakers and stakeholders were guided to ensure valuable resources were effectively utilized and preserved (Ali et al., 2021; Shweta et al., 2022). Policymakers continuously monitor the causes of identified risks while focusing on mitigating and remediating existing vulnerabilities to ensure optimal business operations. Ali et al. (2021) and Shweta et al. (2022) explained that businesses needed to integrate processes to mitigate risks and vulnerabilities and identify tolerable risks for the organization without losing valuable resources. SME owners' identification and evaluation of organizational risks and vulnerabilities motivate proactive mitigation strategies and the implementation of technology-driven disaster preparedness solutions.

This approach fosters robust and sustainable business operational environments in the face of disruptive events. Despite the existing research, there is a notable deficiency in the implementation of technology-driven disaster preparedness among Tennessee SME owners. This gap leads to premature business closures and negatively impacting the state's economy. Researchers like Alexander and Harris (2020) highlighted the importance of innovative preparedness solutions for SMEs, yet there is limited practical application and understanding of these solutions among SME owners.

This exploratory case study specifically addressed these gaps by investigating Tennessee SME owners' understanding and integration of technology-driven disaster preparedness. Using COR theory as the theoretical framework, this study provided valuable insights into resource management strategies enhancing organizational resilience (Cai et al., 2023; Pradhan et al., 2024). Through semi-structured interviews, the study collected in-depth data on SME owners and managers' innovative and technology-driven preparedness solutions implementation and integration of disaster risk procedures.

Furthermore, the study underscored the necessity of effective, technology-driven disaster preparedness to secure data environments, ensure continuous monitoring, and safeguard business reputations (Ali et al., 2021; Green, 2023; Shweta et al., 2022; T. Oyama et al., 2021). By addressing the critical gaps in the current literature. This research highlighted the practical importance of implementing disaster preparedness solutions and providing a roadmap for future studies exploring innovative strategies and emerging solutions for SME owners while minimizing financial expenses and mitigating risks (Ali et al., 2021; Shweta et al., 2022). This study contributed to understanding the challenges faced by Tennessee SME owners before and after disastrous events and offers strategies promoting the advantages of disaster preparedness.

Researchers should continue exploring these in-depth and innovative preparedness strategies to support SME owners in building resilient businesses capable of withstanding and recovering from disasters. This study highlighted the significance of implementing disaster preparedness solutions to tackle the challenges faced by Tennessee SME owners before and after disastrous events. Chapter 3 then outlines the research method and design, population sample, study procedures, data analysis, assumptions, limitations, delimitations, and ethical assurance.

The Research Approach

This chapter outlines the qualitative exploratory case study methodology employed to investigate how SME owners in Tennessee implement disaster preparedness solutions. This methodology directly addresses the literature gaps identified in Chapter 2 by examining the specific challenges and strategies related to the adoption of technology-driven disaster preparedness solutions in SMEs (Bloomberg, 2022; Keidel et al., 2021). The qualitative exploratory case study design, guided by the COR theory, provides a framework for understanding how SME owners preserve and manage resources during disruptive events (Hobfoll, 1989).

Therefore, building on the gaps identified in Chapter 2, this chapter describes the research design and rationale, emphasizing its alignment with the study's problem, purpose, and research questions. The chapter also details the target population, sampling strategy, data collection methods, and thematic analysis approach. Ethical considerations, assumptions, and limitations of the study are also discussed for a transparent and rigorous study. By using semi-structured interviews with SME owners and stakeholders, this chapter demonstrates how the methodology addresses the study's core research questions. The chosen approach facilitates an in-depth exploration of resource challenges and disaster preparedness strategies, contributing to both theoretical and practical insights.

The problem addressed in this study was Tennessee SME owners face challenges when implementing innovative disaster preparedness solutions, which could often result in early business closures, job losses, and negative effects on the state's economy (Coates et al., 2019; J. Ha et al., 2022; Sarmiento et al., 2019; T. Oyama et al., 2021). The purpose of this qualitative exploratory case study was to examine how the implementation of innovative disaster preparedness solutions by Tennessee SME owners, using mitigatory strategies against the challenges faced, will enhance business resilience and facilitate effective responses against disasters.

The study aimed to address the following research questions: (a) How do Tennessee SME owners implement innovative disaster preparedness solutions to address challenges while preserving valuable resources? (b) How do Tennessee SME owners integrate effective procedures to remediate challenging barriers or resource constraints that continue to hinder the implementation of technology-driven disaster preparedness solutions? (c) In what ways do Tennessee SME owners and the incident response workforce embrace an innovative technology-driven disaster preparedness solutions-oriented culture within their organization? (d) How do Tennessee SME owners integrate COR theoretical principles and corollaries within organizations to preserve valuable resources by implementing innovative disaster preparedness solutions?

The research questions focused on understanding how Tennessee SME owners implement innovative disaster preparedness solutions to address challenges in preserving valuable resources. These included: (a) how SME owners integrate effective procedures to overcome barriers; (b) how they foster a culture oriented toward technology-driven disaster preparedness; and (c) how they apply the COR theoretical principles to preserve resources (Bloomberg, 2022; L. Karlı et al., 2022).

The chosen methodology, involving semi-structured interviews and thematic analysis, allows for an in-depth examination of these questions by capturing detailed insights from SME owners, managers, incident response teams, and stakeholders. This approach ensures that the constructs are thoroughly discussed, modified, and confirmed, addressing the literature gaps and providing a comprehensive understanding of the implementation strategies and challenges Tennessee SME owners face (Kekeya, 2021).

Chapter 3 explored the study using a qualitative research methodology and a case study design to conclude and analyze research findings from the data collected. Additionally, Chapter 3 elaborated on why qualitative research methodology was a suitable choice to investigate the need for more technology-driven disaster preparedness solutions among SME owners in Tennessee. The study was validated by explaining the appropriateness of an exploratory case study over other qualitative research method designs (Bloomberg, 2022). Subsequently, a description of the characteristics of the sample population compatible with the study was identified. In addition, suitable interview instruments aligning with this exploratory case study design were identified and selected.

Research Methodology and Design

The qualitative research methodology was the most appropriate methodological approach, aligning effectively with the investigation's following phases, an investigation that adhered to a sequential process (Bloomberg, 2022; Mohajan, 2018). The qualitative research methodology was also chosen to incorporate investigative measures involving humans, aiming to understand their experiences. Analysis software tools were utilized to interpret and analyze findings, definitions, and procedures derived from data collected from SME owners and managers as participants.

The study was conducted in a naturalistic manner, emphasizing qualitative data and focusing on words rather than numerical data (Mohajan, 2018). Qualitative research methodology involves social interactions through interviews and documentation to determine the 'how' and 'why.' Qualitative research methodology systematically indicates circumstances from the participant's perspective or population being studied, generating ideas and theories based on the research questions developed for the study.

Creswell and Creswell (2017) described qualitative research as an effective methodology observed within a natural setting, which provides researchers with an account of real-life events or incidents. The meanings of past or existing events do not apply, as qualitative research indicates using the study's inductive nature. The exploratory nature of the study, coupled with the case study design, led to actionable insights for SME owners and managers in several ways.

First, the qualitative research methodology allowed for a deep and comprehensive understanding of the challenges and strategies related to disaster preparedness in SMEs. On the other hand, a quantitative research methodology was not considered suitable for the study because its focus on measurable attributes did not align with the study's need for contributory findings and interpretations. Furthermore, it would not address the specific research questions developed for the study (Hummel-Rossi et al., 2006).

Quantitative research methodology addresses specific research questions for which variables are measurable. The qualitative approach was chosen to deeply explore the experiences, perspectives, and insights of SME owners regarding disaster preparedness and resilience. This approach aligns with the research questions, which aim to understand the nuanced and context-specific strategies employed by SMEs, the challenges they face, and the impact of innovative technologies and training programs on their preparedness efforts. A qualitative method allows for a rich, detailed understanding of these elements, which quantitative methods might not fully capture.

Qualitative research was the appropriate methodology for the study due to its extensive involvement in a broad information-gathering process using different data collection methods, which guided the qualitative researcher in finding solutions to the problem statement. Similarly, qualitative research methodology highlighted the diverse categories and techniques used to create a detailed process (Bloomberg, 2022; Given, 2008). The qualitative researcher determined the reasoning behind using a qualitative research methodology and how it aligns with the research study.

For this study, the qualitative research methodology was used to delve into the human aspects of the research topic and experiences, gathering participants' views, observations, and lessons learned as investigations progressed. The qualitative research methodology addressed, aligned, and elaborated on the problem, purpose, and research questions to identify the study objectives while determining a logical flow of how the study would be conducted.

Equally, the qualitative research methodology prominently employed interview and observation techniques for data gathering (Bloomberg, 2022; Given, 2008). Moreover, F. Ali et al. (2023), Andrade et al. (2022), Asgary et al. (2020), J. Ha et al. (2022), Mishra et al. (2023), and Ruiz-Cantisani et al. (2020)

examined rigorous studies in the area of technology-driven disaster preparedness implementation by SME owners using different research methodologies and designs. The qualitative researcher determined the reasoning behind the selected methodology and how it aligned with the research study.

For this study, a qualitative research methodology was used to explore the human components of the research topic and experiences as investigations proceeded to obtain participants' views, observations, and lessons learned. The qualitative research methodology addressed, aligned, and elaborated on the problem, purpose, and research questions to identify the study objectives while determining a logical flow of how the study would be conducted. Interviewing and observation techniques for data gathering were prominently utilized for the qualitative research methodology (Bloomberg, 2022; Given, 2008).

Researchers considered qualitative and quantitative research methodologies on similar disaster preparedness topics in the past (Eggers, 2020; Lee & Chen, 2021; Sarmiento et al., 2019). However, qualitative research methodology was confirmed as an effective method to explore prospects while determining consequences experienced as challenges SME owners faced due to a lack of implementing technology-driven disaster preparedness solutions (Asgary et al., 2020; Gwon et al., 2022; Hoerold et al., 2021).

Case Study Design

A case study is defined as a specific single or multiple case(s) indicating critical situations by collecting data in different stages using interviews with participants to understand human experiences (Stake, 1978). Case study designs demonstrated how the qualitative research methodology could provide a comprehensive approach, incorporating boundaries through simplified processes and ensuring the research questions are addressed definitively (Kekeya, 2021; Mohajan, 2018; Stake, 1978; Yin, 2018). The case study design is a general term for exploring a group of people or phenomena (Mohajan, 2018).

Additionally, a case study takes time due to its constraining characteristics for one or multiple cases within an environment. The case study targets participants such as a person, population, or organization, focusing on the topic of interest by the qualitative researcher, ensuring boundaries are kept unaltered. Conversely, the case study protocol involves four stages: (a) An outline of the case study; (b) an information-gathering process including participants' data protection, identification, contact credentials, and reminders; (c) research questions; and (d) a detailed explanation of the case study design (Mohajan, 2018; Stake, 1978).

The case study protocol, in its boundaries, specifically distinguishes itself from other studies. The case study process was defined by the content and context of the research, focused on the need for more implementation of disaster preparedness by SME owners, adhering to the data collection protocol, and assessing the integration of innovative solutions (Mohajan, 2018; Stake, 1978). Case studies indicate that a detailed assessment is initiated through data collection.

Moreover, a case study research design addresses several topics and compares diverse study methods and findings (Gomm et al., 2004; Merriam, 1988; Stake, 1978). Case studies entirely depend on inductive thinking, as the qualitative researcher must analyze the collected data. Likewise, different cases focus mainly on people, institutions, organizations, and processes, whereby a case study can be identified in a single case without questions to determine the basis for a case study research design (Mohajan, 2018; Yin, 2018).

A case study research design uses a linear yet iterative approach (Yin, 2018). It is conducted by establishing a plan, selecting a design, preparing to begin collecting data, analyzing the data collected using analysis tools to create themes, and concluding findings through the categorized themes for presentation. The case study design protocol demonstrates how the qualitative researcher follows formal procedures during the research process. Stake (1978) identified two critical points: (a) Determining how the study will be approached by acknowledging the existing tradition, and (b) Understanding an exploratory case study is a different qualitative methodology design.

Exploratory Case Study

An exploratory case study design was selected to indicate "how" and "why" this research needed to be conducted, which identified the importance and setbacks of the study (H. Karlı et al., 2022). The exploratory case study interprets events and existing dynamics to embody features and presents the cohesion of different study projects. The qualitative researcher conducted the study using an exploratory case study research design to collect data using exploratory and investigative methods, analyze the information gathered, and identify solutions to address findings.

The research method and design selected were an excellent fit for this study primarily due to the shared perspective of the participants from whom the data were collected to understand awareness, readiness, and experiences through lessons learned. The exploratory case study also delivered necessary evidence, including an information-gathering path to demonstrate how data were collected, assessed, and construed to provide topics for additional review (H. Karlı et al., 2022).

As the research progressed, the problem, purpose, and research questions the researcher developed led to a distinctive study outcome focusing on information gathering and analysis procedures. Equally, the qualitative exploratory case study adhered to a research protocol divided into five entities: (a) Determination of research design, (b) identification of the existing problem, (c) sampling of participants, (d) information gathering, and (e) data analysis (Pope, 2017). Besides, the exploratory case study will guide the qualitative researcher in delivering an aligned, rigorous, and thorough analysis.

This in-depth exploratory case study will align the research by analyzing the collected data obtained using an investigative approach by integrating research and interview questions with participants (Bloomberg, 2022; Creswell & Creswell, 2017). Therefore, the qualitative exploratory case study was the most appropriate research design to investigate SME owners' need for technology-driven disaster preparedness implementation, determining propositions for strengthening organizational resilience, training the workforce, and integrating technologically innovative solutions.

Alternative Qualitative Research Methodology Designs

Alternative qualitative research methodologies could have been considered for this study, but were not chosen due to the less rigorous and detailed research process compared to the exploratory case study design. The methodologies not considered included narrative inquiry, phenomenology, grounded theory, and ethnography (Bloomberg, 2022; Creswell & Creswell, 2017). Firstly, narrative research design focuses on studying individuals' personal stories to understand their personalities for developmental and psychological purposes (Bloomberg, 2022; Creswell & Creswell, 2017; Hiles & Cermák, 2008; Mohajan, 2018).

Due to the narrative research design, the data-gathering process and its objectives would not fit this study effectively. The phenomenological research method was another design that presented a descriptive and interpretative design merging hermeneutic beliefs explaining how situations appeared, thereby confirming why this study would not be an appropriate design methodology (Bloomberg, 2022; Giorgi & Giorgi, 2008). Following this, grounded theory research design is a robust qualitative approach that originates from a sociological method of data analysis.

It aims to construct a theory through a systematic, inductive, and interactive design methodology. It can be used to conduct interactive inquiries. Data is collected through analyses, and the data collected is assessed from the beginning of the study procedure (Bloomberg, 2022).

Thus, a grounded theory qualitative research design would not be compatible with this study. Ethnography research methodology design covers an in-depth study within sociology and psychological studies, also described as a persistent type of research design (Bengry-Howell & Griffin, 2012; Bloomberg, 2022). Ethnographical research design is defined as the focus on observing participants to deeply understand the culture of a specific social group within society. Through a thorough investigation, the ethnographic research design observes participants' lifestyles and actions to understand perspectives on particular viewpoints.

The ethnographic qualitative research design was not compatible with this exploratory study due to the prolonged information-gathering process, including the qualitative researcher becoming familiar with the cultural environment can lengthen the study extensively (Coates et al., 2019; Gwon et al., 2022; J. Ha et al., 2022; Seong et al., 2023; T. Oyama et al., 2021).

Therefore, the qualitative exploratory case study would be the most appropriate research design to investigate SME owners' need for technology-driven disaster preparedness implementation to determine propositions of strengthening organizational resilience, training the workforce, and integrating technologically innovative solutions.

Research Setting and Data Collection Method

The research documentation setting included contact information of SME owners obtained from publicly listed sources in the greater metropolitan area of Nashville, Tennessee, and LinkedIn posts. Standards for data collection protocol followed a uniform and consistent process. This involved sending recruitment electronic mails to SME owners to enroll participants from whom data was collected using semi-structured interviews (Adame et al., 2020; Schroeder et al., 2024).

Data were collected using semi-structured interviews (N=8), then categorized into small groups for manageability across multiple organizations in diverse industries. Participant recruitment criteria included SME owners, managers, stakeholders, or incident response team members who were 18 years or older and owned or managed a business with 10-500 employees. Participants should have encountered a disastrous event within the last two years. The semi-structured interviews with these participants were recorded, transcribed, and analyzed using thematic analysis to identify what needed to be cross-referenced for validation. These interviews were conducted with SME owners (N=8) across different technology, healthcare, security, and housing industries.

Data Collection Protocol

The data collection protocol followed a uniform process of asking participants similar interview questions; each semi-structured interview lasted 45-60 minutes. Data collection was performed using video and audio recording, then transcribed, followed by coding and analyzing the information gathered using identified thematic words and phrases with NVivo qualitative data analysis software, Version 12 (Adame et al., 2020; Alexander & Harris, 2020; Andrade et al., 2022; Palinkas et al., 2021; Schroeder et al., 2024). Thematic analysis, including coding strategies to identify patterns, ensured that key data were systematically captured and analyzed. Upon theme categorization, sentence segmentations were analyzed for coding purposes. The data collection process from participants is illustrated in the figure below to present a logical flow.

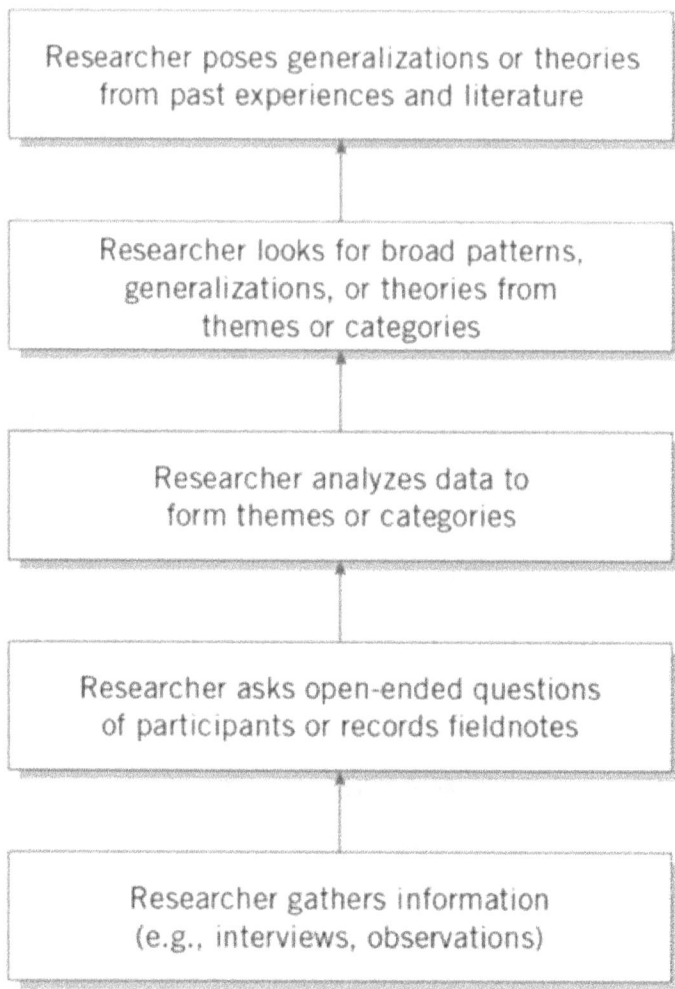

Figure 1. Visual Logic of the Exploratory Research Design.

Note. The figure above illustrates the initiation of the exploratory study following data collection from participants such as SME owners, managers, the incident response workforce, and stakeholders using semi-structured interviews to categorize them into themes (Creswell & Creswell, 2017). These themes were advanced into patterns and theories, identifying different endpoints for the study.

Population and Sample

The population of this study consisted of SME owners and managers in the greater Nashville area of Tennessee, representing various industries, including manufacturing, healthcare, technology, and retail. The region chosen was due to its diverse economic landscape and recent experiences with disastrous events, which make it a suitable context for examining disaster preparedness solutions. The population and sample for this qualitative exploratory case study entailed participants from industries such as technology, healthcare, supply chain, education, and hospitality.

The participants for this exploratory case study were adults over 18 years of age, male, female, able, disabled, SME owners, stakeholders, leaders, incident response workforce, and from different races to ensure all participants were represented throughout the study (Creswell & Creswell, 2017). The recruited participants for this exploratory case study were SME owners in business settings with 10-500 employees and determined the state of readiness towards disastrous events or lessons learned was existent.

Detailed Description of the Population

The target population included SME owners and managers with 10-500 employees. The diversity in industry types and specific focus on organizations within Tennessee provided a broad yet contextually rich understanding of the challenges and strategies for disaster preparedness, whereby SME owners implement strategies that contribute to the local economy, promoting employment and economic activity in the area (Smith & Anderson, 2020).

Justification for the Sample Size and Sampling Method

The principle of data saturation justified the chosen sample size. Data saturation was achieved when no new information or themes emerged from the data, ensuring that the sample size of eight participants was sufficient and captured the necessary insights (Guest et al., 2006; Hennink et al., 2016). This sample size aligned with qualitative research standards, often recommending smaller, focused samples to provide in-depth insights (Creswell, 2013). The purposive sampling method was employed to select participants who experienced disastrous events in the last two years, ensuring that the study captured relevant and recent experiences with disaster preparedness solutions (Bloomberg, 2022).

Data saturation was achieved from the reliability and validity of the results by cross-verifying information using member checking of the transcribed data collected by participants (Hennink et al., 2016). This rigorous analytical process led to actionable perceptions to inform best practices, policy recommendations, and strategic interventions for SME owners and managers. Detailed data comparison and classification were essential and adhered to establishing data collection protocols (Gillani et al., 2022).

Data collected was manually categorized into three classifications and defined using a combined theoretical view of consumer experience and a Service-Dominant Logic (SDL; W. Wang et al., 2022; Yogia et al., 2024). SDL's theoretical approach aimed at value co-creation procedures and identified unessential resources (W. Wang et al., 2022; Yogia et al., 2024). Initiative themes were assessed to eliminate duplicate information and titles through text assessments (W. Wang et al., 2022).

Eligibility Criteria

To be eligible for participation in the study, individuals should have fulfilled participation criteria, which were as follows: (a) 18 years and older; (b) SME owners, managers, stakeholders, or incident response workforce of organizations in the greater Nashville area; (c) Have experienced disastrous events within the last two years; and (d) Be willing to participate in semi-structured interviews and share their experiences and strategies related to disaster preparedness. These criteria ensured that the participants had a direct and recent experience with the challenges and strategies associated with disaster preparedness in SMEs.

Explanation of the Geographic Focus

The geographic focus on the greater Nashville area is due to the region's recent history of significant disastrous events, including floods, tornadoes, and infrastructure failures (Tennessee Emergency Management Agency, 2021). This focus provided a relevant context for examining innovative disaster preparedness solutions as SMEs in the greater Nashville area faced and responded to these challenges. By studying SMEs in the identified specific region, the research aimed to collect highly relevant data to the local context while offering broader implications for similar regions facing comparable risks and challenges (Smith & Anderson, 2020).

Sample Population

Participant recruitment and selection for this exploratory case study were initiated upon IRB approval. Participants were contacted through email, electronic means, and social media platforms like LinkedIn. Potential participants were selected based on their experience and expertise to ensure credible and valid recommendations.

The exploratory case study utilized purposeful sampling to select participants, ensuring a reliable structure by randomly selecting a specific number based on a fraction defined by the qualitative researcher (Bloomberg, 2022; Creswell & Creswell, 2017). Bloomberg (2022) defined purposeful sampling as selecting specific participants, events, and processes with a detailed strategy for accessing data relevant to the study. Recruitment and selection of participants for this exploratory case study commenced following IRB approval. Participants were contacted electronically using social media platforms like LinkedIn and through distributed electronic mail.

The researcher ensured that no coercion or undue influence was exerted. The population sample involved male and female participants who met established inclusion and exclusion criteria while representing diverse intentions for the integration of innovative disaster preparedness solutions for cities in the greater Nashville area and had experienced a disastrous event within the last two years (Adame et al., 2020; Matthews-Trigg et al., 2019). In addition, the inclusion criteria for recruiting potential participants included: (a) you are 18 years or older; (b) you own a business with employees ranging between 1-500 in the Greater Nashville Metro Area; (c) you have encountered a disastrous event within the last two years; and (d) you have or considered implementing technology-driven disaster preparedness measures.

Participants were selected according to the nature of their roles within the organization, such as SME owners, managers, incident response team leaders, or stakeholders from diverse industries. All participants were fluent in English; interviews or surveys were conducted in a different language for data-collection purposes, and the information gathered was translated into English and transcribed. The sampling selection process for the study ensured that SMEs are organizations with 10 – 500 employees. This played an essential role in defining vulnerable states towards disruptive events within business environments, emphasizing the criticality of disaster preparedness implementation.

Sampling Design and Size

Another sampling method for recruiting participants in this qualitative exploratory case study was snowball sampling, which was used alongside purposeful sampling. Snowball sampling was considered an alternative approach for discovering and recruiting participants (Bloomberg, 2022; Creswell & Creswell, 2017). The sampling method selected for this qualitative exploratory case study was a purposeful sampling for recruiting participants, whereby snowball sampling was also considered to find additional participants (Bloomberg, 2022; Creswell & Creswell, 2017).

Purposeful sampling was the method used to strategically recruit participants, determined by who was the best fit for the exploratory case study. Sampling decision criteria were met for ethical constraints and availability (Creswell & Creswell, 2017). The estimated target population size was defined as (N=8) for semi-structured interviews (Andrade et al., 2022; Pope, 2017; Schroeder et al., 2024).

The sample size population focused on SME owners, managers, stakeholders, and incident response workforce to ensure that semi-structured interviews used as data collection procedures were accurate, practical, and relevant to the study (Andrade et al., 2022; Pope, 2017; Schroeder et al., 2024). Minimally defined sampling groups represented the larger population (Kekeya, 2021). Therefore, when selecting a sample population for the research topic, the qualitative researcher considered specific essential factors: (a) sampling strategy effectiveness, (b) defined sampling size, (c) population sample group leader identification, and (d) participants' information.

Sampling Frame

Purposeful sampling was employed to recruit SME owners and managers as participants for the study. Recruited participants were informed of the study's objectives and goals as part of the semi-structured interview questionnaires. Online consent was obtained prior to interviews to ensure adherence to ethical guidelines. Recruited participants also suggested other SME owners and leaders in the greater Nashville area who had experienced a disastrous event as potential candidates for the semi-structured interviews. This recommendation served as a form of random sampling to ensure diverse perspectives.

Instrumentation

Data collection instrumentation techniques were integrated to gather information for this qualitative exploratory case study using the research questions organized in an established format (Creswell & Creswell, 2017; Salmia, 2023). An effective instrument, also identified as a tool, provided details about the research and was integrated to prove truth and rigor. The research instruments selected were equally reliable and valid. The qualitative researcher also considered a human research instrument that confirmed the study direction by recruiting participants, collecting data, assessing the information collected, and summarizing the analyzed data to simplify the codes developed for better comprehension.

Participants for this qualitative exploratory case study included SME owners, managers, the incident response workforce, and stakeholders. Human qualitative research instruments were employed for an in-depth study addressing the problem statement (Creswell & Creswell, 2017; Salmia, 2023). The data collected presented reliability and validity by adhering to a well-established plan and following detailed protocols.

The reliability of the instruments confirmed their validity and dependability in gathering detailed information. The qualitative researcher maintained the same instruments and research materials throughout the study to ensure consistent results. Any changes could have affected the reliability and validity of the data findings, leading to compromised outcomes if new instruments were integrated. Providing sample items collected with a specific instrument helped readers understand the integrated items and their usage (Creswell & Creswell, 2017).

Bloomberg (2022) and Salmia (2023) concluded that qualitative researchers had strengths and weaknesses when using human instruments for data collection. After selecting the research instrument(s) for this qualitative exploratory case study, semi-structured interviews were utilized to collect data. Data collected was recorded from the interview questions and transcribed following the data-gathering process (Salmia, 2023).

The qualitative researcher used one or more methods for investigative data gathering, depending on the study's problem statement, and ensured the instrument was implemented effectively for data collection and detailed analysis. The research outcomes maximized the attainment of study objectives, adhering to the data collection purpose and research methodology. The study employed a qualitative, exploratory case study approach to examine the need for SME owners to implement technology-driven disaster preparedness solutions.

Using a purposive sampling strategy guided by the COR theory, the research selected eight participants from the greater Nashville area who had experienced a disastrous event in the last two years. Data were collected through semi-structured interviews, transcribed using Otter.ai, and thematically analyzed with NVivo software (Bazeley & Jackson, 2013; Bloomberg, 2022; Keidel et al., 2021). The study identified factors impeding the adoption of these solutions and targeted SME owners, managers, incident response teams, and stakeholders from organizations with 1-500 employees.

Semi-structured interviews with participants ensured that the proposed constructs were discussed, modified, and confirmed with intensity to establish the exploratory case study components. Dalkin et al. (2020) conducted a realist evaluation to explore the health impact of welfare advice services, utilizing NVivo software to aid in the complex theory generation, refinement, and testing process. The study highlighted how NVivo facilitated systematic coding, categorization, and the identification of patterns and themes within qualitative data.

NVivo's advanced features, such as text search and visualization tools, enhanced transparency and collaboration among the research team by tracking changes and linking memos. Although it did not reduce the time required for data analysis, NVivo made the process more efficient and rigorous, ultimately providing deeper insights and clearer justification of findings. This case study demonstrates NVivo's valuable role in managing and analyzing qualitative data, contributing to the robustness and reliability of the research outcomes.

The research highlighted the necessity for SME owners to adopt innovative, technology-driven disaster preparedness solutions to mitigate events that disrupt business resilience and revenue growth (L. Karlı et al., 2022). It contributed to the existing literature by detailing procedures for implementing these solutions and ensuring data saturation through a clear data collection protocol that maintained confidentiality and anonymity (Bloomberg, 2022; Gennari, 2022; Hennink et al.,

2016; Mohajan, 2018). Reliability was confirmed using the human instrument to indicate repetitive behavior following the developed technique and evaluated according to established constructs (Creswell & Creswell, 2017).

The findings underscored the importance of specific constructs such as financial resources, policy development, and integrated disaster response frameworks, which were indicated as critical elements for the successful implementation of technology-driven disaster preparedness solutions for SME owners (Kekeya, 2021).

Semi-structured Interviews

Semi-structured interviews were used to collect data for this qualitative exploratory case study using an unstructured approach, whereby the outcome was not predictable (Salmia, 2023). The qualitative researcher needed help identifying considerations explicitly defined for standardized instruments; however, objects and stages were identified using interview questions developed and used by the qualitative researcher throughout the data collection process. Semi-structured interviews were used to gather data from recruited participants.

The data collection process was conducted in a warm, friendly, open demeanor while listening to and recording participants' experiences with no interruptions or biases using an iterative process.

Interview Process

The semi-structured and focus group interviews followed an established process, namely: (a) participant selection; (b) specific details that followed set interview questions; (c) the interview process was begun; (d) confirmed the end of the interview and the summary of the data collected was closed; (e) interview outcomes in written notes were documented; and (f) the interviewee participant's details and experience were confirmed (Salmia, 2023).

The qualitative researcher documented reactions during data collection, knowledge and fact findings, educational level, employment status, contact details, and role verification procedures of recruited participants. Interviewing was identified as a prevalent source of data collection for the qualitative exploratory case study as an instrument for information gathering. Key elements included quickly understanding what was relevant to the recruited participants during the study (Bloomberg, 2022; Salmia, 2023).

The researcher ceased exploration once data saturation was achieved (Hennink et al., 2016). At the point of data saturation, decision-making and information analysis continued to conclude the findings with thorough explanations. The qualitative researcher faced challenges as a human instrument, such as maintaining consistency and neutrality throughout the study, avoiding biases, and refraining from making assumptions about the data collected. Additionally, the qualitative researcher completed documentation, journaling, written notes, assessments, and study presentations.

The research instruments used for data collection were systematically arranged, demonstrating their effectiveness in fulfilling the investigative purposes of the study using the established interview questions, which have been added as Appendix A, Research Instrument.

Study Procedures

The study procedures followed a series of phases aligned with the data collection protocol designed to specify what data to collect, when and where to gather it, from whom, and whether the process could be replicated, conducted, and explained. The research process included the following steps:

1. An application was submitted to the National University Institutional Review Board (IRB) for approval to begin, including data collection from prospective participants. The IRB application was submitted on May 31, 2024.

2. Participants were carefully recruited to ensure they were small business leaders in the greater Nashville Area.

3. Following IRB approval on June 26, 2024, participant recruitment emails and LinkedIn messages were sent to SME owners using purposive random sampling alongside postings on social media.

4. Recruited participants were informed about the study's scope and were asked to verbally consent to voluntary participation and guided through the ethical standards by the researcher.

5. Semi-structured interviews were conducted to obtain participants' consent for recording audio or video data. The researcher ensured that all participants were reminded of their freedom to withdraw from the interview at any time.

6. Semi-structured interviews were held via Zoom meetings using interview questions. A copy of the instrumentation interview research questions was included in Appendix A.

7. According to the established data collection protocol, all participants were asked the same set of interview questions, with sessions lasting 45-60 minutes.

8. The recorded interviews were transcribed using Otter.ai and sent to participants for member checking.

9. The collected and transcribed data were forwarded to the participants for member checking prior to coding and analysis, allowing them to confirm the accuracy or provide any missing information.

10. Data coding of the transcribed material commenced after participants reviewed the transcripts, using NVivo software for analysis.

11. The data were analyzed and categorized into sub-themes and themes using NVivo software to identify patterns and document a conclusive summary of findings.

12. All data collected, coded, and analyzed were securely stored on a hard drive, and I was the only one who could access the securely stored data kept in a locked safe.

13. Additionally, all data collected were anonymized to protect participants' confidentiality through the use of pseudonyms and will be securely destroyed after three years.

14. Upon study completion, data closure was submitted to the National University IRB.

Data Analysis

Data were collected using semi-structured interviews, transcribed, and assessed to ensure reliability and consistency were prevalent, and proceeded to establish categories, sub-themes, and improved themes (J. Ha et al., 2022; Schroeder et al., 2024). The data collection protocol was guided through analysis using diverse information for interpretation and marking an in-depth categorical mapping of effective and targeted relevant information (Gillani et al., 2022). Data analysis was conducted using codes to integrate and identify different stages of the study while connecting all parts and sections.

Consequently, qualitative data analysis outcomes were used to identify specific research elements to explore findings (Saldaña, 2009). The qualitative data analysis process identified patterns and themes within the data collected to exude their importance in supporting the exploratory case study. The qualitative exploratory case study presented the process and stages of assessing the collected data to develop a precise and thorough analysis using coding methods to be categorized into themes (Creswell & Creswell, 2017; Yüzlü, 2023).

The assessed data analysis was extracted from the transcribed information, whereby the qualitative researcher proceeded to document findings for presentation and through narrative reporting. The data collected was examined to obtain a focused process specifying relevant information to the study. Data were analyzed using analysis programming tools to assist with categorization, organization, storage, and findability (Creswell & Creswell, 2017).

The qualitative researcher continuously re-evaluated the codes developed to effectively analyze the large amounts of data collected using the NVivo software tool, whereby the data analysis process was rigorous and iterative for adequate maintenance against conflict of interest and to protect participants. The qualitative researcher analyzed the collected data inductively to develop patterns and categorize codes into sub-themes and themes from the bottom up and then deductively from the top down (Alexander & Harris, 2020; Riaz & Khan, 2024). Themes indicated cross-referenced data to determine if relevant information existed to support the exploratory case study for each theme or if additional information was needed.

The strategies for the analyzed data collected were categorized into themes chronologically. The process surrounding theme creation provided a step-by-step procedure outlining clarity for the assessed data (Vaismoradi & Snelgrove, 2019). Sub-themes were developed with similar categorization constructs and themes.

The data analysis process was iterative, with the researcher continuously evaluating and organizing codes to group related codes and identify patterns within the coded data. Coding was an iterative and systematic procedure to analyze all the collected and categorized information, relying on the participants' definitions and acknowledgment of the recorded and documented data. Furthermore, the researcher adhered to coding procedures to develop categories and themes through data analysis, ensuring a detailed rendering of participants' interview recordings for each data collection setting.

The qualitative researcher developed a narrative by conducting semi-structured interviews to collect data, which was then transcribed, coded, and analyzed. The findings were presented using detailed tables, figures, and charts. Accurate and excellent research was concluded from efficient coding of collected data through written notes and journal documentation, and transcribed analysis of research interviews (Saldaña, 2009).

Codes were categorized into three different entities: (a) Expected codes indicated the awaited data findings; (b) Surprising codes were identified as code findings and not predicted or different from the start of the research, whereby the results surprised the qualitative researcher; (c) Unusual conceptual interest codes would retrigger participants from past events during the data collection process and disturb participants through the reporting of loss of valuable assets after a disruptive event was avoided; (d) Predetermined codes developed by researchers using a qualitative codebook table outlining its use and identify each code's meaning for an in-depth meaning of each code; and (e) Visual images provided by participant(s) by drafting images or pictures reflecting cultural advancements (Creswell & Creswell, 2017).

The categories, which the qualitative researcher labeled as sub-themes, were further organized into themes based on their similarities and relationships to extract meaningful reports. (Vaismoradi & Snelgrove, 2019). Upon finalizing theme development, the researcher documented a coherent report of the exploratory case study observations. The report detailed the information findings and the achievement of data saturation. Throughout the data-collecting process, the researcher relied on traceability and abstraction with the selected research data collection methods (Bloomberg, 2022; Ešić et al., 2021).

The qualitative exploratory case study determined whether data saturation was achieved following data collection from various sources using selected instrumentation and materials (Hennink et al., 2016). Additionally, the qualitative researcher ensured participants' privacy by adhering to ethical standards and using anonymous data to promote the confidentiality of private information. (Bloomberg, 2022). An outline of the data analysis process involved multiple stages: (a) Data collected was arranged and transcribed from recorded interviews and written notes highlighting information according to origin; (b) the meaning of the data collected through the tone of recorded interviews was determined to establish an overall understanding of the data collected; and (c) further documentation of all comments were drafted after every semi-structured interview to be defined as sketched ideas (Creswell & Creswell, 2017).

The research study focused on ensuring that data saturation was achieved once rich and in-depth data was collected, and no additional information was expected to be used to develop new themes (Hennink et al., 2016; Kekeya, 2021). The qualitative researcher's role in this study was to conduct the research ethically and rigorously, avoiding objective or disinterested information gathering (Bloomberg, 2022; Iphofen & Tolich,

2018). Through coding, the researcher employed analytical objectives, guided by their perception of the collected data, to categorize the information based on similarities.

This qualitative exploratory case study contributed to the existing literature by detailing participants' processes of implementing innovative and technology-driven disaster preparedness solutions (Gennari, 2022). The researcher was immersed in the research and paid attention to any information that may evoke emotional responses from SME owners and employees, potentially affecting their values or demeanor. To help the qualitative researcher avoid biases and errors, it was crucial to refrain from applying assumptions to the analysis or findings. The study topic was approached without personal or professional biases, effectively addressing the problem statement.

Assumptions

The assumptive beliefs that could have influenced the information-gathering procedures as the qualitative researcher began data collection involved SME owners' lack of innovative technology-driven disaster preparedness solutions implementation, which were mitigated by acknowledging the biases and documenting the researcher's bias (Bloomberg, 2022). The collected data were categorized using research questions to analyze trends, themes, and patterns while avoiding biases through a deductive approach. In this manner, the researcher extracted facts from the exploratory case study to avoid assumptions and establish credible, meaningful, detailed, and efficient research (Boutmaghzoute & Moustaghfir, 2021).

The assessment used various instruments, such as semi-structured interviews, to evaluate the implementation of technology-driven disaster preparedness solutions, how these would increase resilience, and, if not, what SME owners would rely on (Bloomberg, 2022; Ešić et al., 2021). Participants also shared different interpretations of the existing lack of technology-driven disaster preparedness solutions (Bloomberg, 2022). Participants were recruited from diverse industries, thereby bringing in multiple views and perspectives, uncovering untapped objectives, and ensuring a rigorous and thorough study was achieved. Additionally, personal perspectives and beliefs introduced challenges by imposing assumptions on this exploratory case study.

Limitations

The study anticipated several limitations, particularly concerning participant recruitment and data collection during the recovery phase following a disastrous event. Given the sensitivity of circumstances post-disaster, it was challenging for SME owners to participate in interviews, especially if they had experienced significant losses (J. Ha et al., 2022; Van Brown, 2020). Furthermore, disaster-affected environments presented physical safety and psychological risks to all involved, affecting data collection (J. Ha et al., 2022; Van Brown, 2020).

SME owners' responsiveness was also impacted by the devastation, death, and property losses they faced (J. Ha et al., 2022; Van Brown, 2020). These factors necessitated caution to avoid oversimplification and often required additional in-depth research. Other limitations were related to organizational size and the knowledge necessary for SME owners to implement technology-driven disaster preparedness solutions (Bloomberg, 2022; Mohajan, 2018).

Additionally, qualitative research faced general limitations concerning population and sampling representation (Bloomberg, 2022; Mohajan, 2018). Researchers acknowledged and mitigated these by addressing biases and participant reactivity, where participants may have had difficulty pivoting as interviewees. The qualitative researcher also confronted and investigated the study's limitations to understand how they would be interpreted and what outcomes to expect.

This approach helped readers discern if the research was beneficial within its identified context and facilitated information transferability. The limitations were mitigated by demonstrating authenticity and control over the study while ensuring ethical assurance to protect participants' well-being (Bloomberg, 2022; Mohajan, 2018). As a result, the findings might not have fully captured the experiences and perspectives of all SME owners (S. Ha et al., 2022).

Furthermore, participants who volunteered for the study might have had specific characteristics, such as a higher awareness of disaster preparedness, which could have influenced the results. This meant that the results might not have been generalizable to all SME owners, particularly those who might have been less aware or less engaged in disaster preparedness efforts. The study context, such as the specific economic and environmental conditions in Tennessee, might have influenced the findings.

This implied that the results might not have been applicable to SME owners in regions with different economic, environmental, or regulatory conditions. To enhance the generalizability of the findings, future research should aim to increase sample size and diversity by including a larger and more varied sample of SME owners from different regions and industries. Employing random sampling methods can help reduce selection bias and ensure a more balanced representation of participants. Conducting similar studies in different contexts and comparing the results will motivate the identification of whether the findings are consistent across various settings.

Delimitations

Delimitations were defined as the original selections for the overall design of the research, which could not be identified at the beginning of data collection but instead after the completion of the study (Bloomberg, 2022). Delimitations followed, identifying the study boundaries and how the methodology design was selected while rejecting alternative methods that could have been integrated (Bloomberg, 2022; Mohajan, 2018).

For example, parameters like the location of the study— in this case, the greater Nashville area in Tennessee—were considered delimitations. Delimitations guided the study by confirming why certain aspects of the research problem could not be studied and were not intended to be covered. They addressed all inquiries by remaining open, avoiding confusion for the reader, and adhering to the study's transparent and holistic approach.

Delimitations also aligned the theoretical framework with the problem statement, purpose statement, and research questions, thereby developing a coherent, rigorous, and in-depth study that clarified what was to be included.

Ethical Assurances

With the developed research questions, the study aimed to understand the challenges faced by Tennessee SME owners and the lack of implementation of innovative disaster preparedness solutions to mitigate disaster risk, particularly after experiencing disruptive events. Ethical and moral expectations were met by obtaining verbal and written consent from the recruited participants, including approval from the National University IRB, before initiating any data collection process. All collected data were securely stored on a thumb drive in a secured safety container to protect participants from future harm, with plans to destroy the data after three years.

Ethical guidelines were adhered to during the recruitment of SME owner participants, using informed consent during the information-gathering process from communities and businesses (Hintz & Dean, 2020). The qualitative researcher aimed to protect participants' identities while establishing trust in the digital environment, following strong ethical precautions due to the rise in internet fraud statewide, primarily through social media resources (Khurana et al., 2022). Informed consent clearly outlined the risks and benefits of the study, as well as its nature and scope. This assured that participants comprehended the study procedures and how data would be collected with complete transparency.

The qualitative researcher adhered to fundamental ethical principles outlined by Eckstein (2003), including (a) respecting participants, (b) beneficence by treating participants ethically, and (c) ensuring justice by setting practical boundaries upon obtaining informed written and verbal consent. Eckstein (2003) emphasized the significance of behavioral studies and established practices by summarizing these principles. Caruth (2015) noted examples of ethical guidelines, such as the World Medical Association's Declaration of Helsinki in 1964, the Food and Drug Law of 1906—which was the first law in America regulating food and drugs—and the Nuremberg Code of 1947, which established ethical standards for research on human subjects (p. 25-26).

The basic moral principles documented by the Commission outlined the process for addressing ethical problems and resolutions related to research involving human participants (Eckstein, 2003). The qualitative researcher assured participants of the protection of their data privacy, confirming how private information was to be protected by adhering to the ethical assurance for this study, which was achieved by using anonymous data to promote the confidentiality of private information (Bloomberg, 2022). Caruth (2015) further explained how ethics were reported as far back as the Greek philosophical study of morality, referencing the importance of decisions and behaviors.

Ethics are defined as a research category related to choosing right from wrong, behaviorally protecting human participants, and preparing the data for analysis. For ethical purposes, inclusivity was important for all voices from all backgrounds and businesses for this exploratory case study, which was documented, analyzed, and reported while protecting the participants' privacy and dignity (Pope, 2017). Confidentiality and anonymity were achieved by creating an environment in which the qualitative researcher could collect data with integrity using the selected research methods and design.

All collected information was transcribed, documented, and reported truthfully to benefit small business organizations from which the data were collected. Data collected, transcribed, coded, and analyzed were securely stored, adhering to the data privacy protection protocol developed to protect participants' confidentiality and to ensure access was limited to the qualitative researcher (Iphofen & Tolich, 2018). The importance of ethical values includes protecting participants against harm, ensuring data privacy, and respecting their autonomy. The qualitative researcher's dispositions included being friendly and respectful, paying attention to details, and possessing knowledge of the topic, which was considered a virtue of ethics.

IRB Approval Process

The qualitative exploratory case study data collection process began following National University IRB approval. Ethics in research were demonstrated through responsibility and ownership between the qualitative researcher and participants (Bloomberg, 2022; Caruth, 2015). The IRB committee was relied upon as an expert in the ethical research environment, whereby the researcher was considered to be at the initial stage of the ethical procedure.

The IRB approved the study before data collection began to ensure that interviewing human subjects with research work was accomplished accurately (Pope, 2017). Once the IRB was approved, recruiting participants was preceded by data collection using semi-structured interviews from the sample population. Ethical behavior was followed during data collection procedures and stopped when a participant identified an uncomfortable situation that arose to demonstrate an understanding of moral boundaries.

Participants felt comfortable throughout the entire interview and focus group process. The qualitative researcher gained verbal and written consent from participants and demonstrated an understanding of ethical guidelines upon recruiting participants (Iphofen & Tolich, 2018). The established protection procedures are intended to avoid harm to the recruited population following IRB approval.

The data collection methods were observed and verified, emphasizing the promotion of participants' data protection following IRB regulations (Pope, 2017). As it applies to this study, the qualitative exploratory case study was not intended to result in an expected or predetermined outcome. Upon approval, following the recruitment of participants, data gathering was the next phase and was only done using specifically selected methods for this study.

The qualitative research methodology and design indicated an unstructured approach, guided by individual experiences, to understand the intentions behind the analyzed data findings (Shiferaw et al., 2022). The qualitative exploratory case study aligned with the problem statement, purpose statement, and research questions to ensure the information collected addressed the research problem (Pope, 2017). The study collected detailed and relevant information from participants and ensured the case study research components were interlinked for a holistically thorough approach (Bloomberg, 2022; Creswell & Creswell, 2017).

The qualitative exploratory case study revealed that the sample population provided rich data and in-depth information through semi-structured interviews. This approach made the process manageable among participants, ranging from one to eight individuals (Pope, 2017). For qualitative research purposes, data were collected from a participant, one industry, one company, or one singular department within an organization, identified as a case study characteristic. Participants were assured and provided guidance, adhering to the data collection protocol. Data collected from the participants was analyzed, coded, and categorized into themes (Pope, 2017).

Data analysis coding ensured themes were developed for conclusive findings from the data gathered, and the results were stored in qualitative data. Future research is recommended to continue investigating how SME owners should effectively adopt innovative and technology-driven disaster preparedness solutions against increasingly diverse challenges pre- and post-disastrous impacts (Asgary et al., 2020). This study focused on

Tennessee SME owners' adoption of technology-driven disaster preparedness solutions to protect investments, aligning with COR theory, and presents the research findings in Chapter 4, ensuring the trustworthiness of the collected data.

Key Themes and Observations

The themes developed following coded data analysis were categorized under the research questions and explained in detail. The themes and sub-themes created during the analysis were grouped under the research questions, elaborating on the foundation of trustworthiness and identifying the study's credibility, transferability, dependability, and confirmability standards (Bloomberg, 2022). The problem addressed in this study was Tennessee SME owners face challenges when implementing innovative disaster preparedness solutions, which could often result in early business closures, job losses, and negative effects on the state's economy (Coates et al., 2019; J. Ha et al., 2022; Sarmiento et al., 2019; T. Oyama et al., 2021).

The purpose of this qualitative exploratory case study was to examine how the implementation of innovative disaster preparedness solutions by Tennessee SME owners through mitigatory strategies against the challenges faced will enhance business resilience and facilitate effective responses against disasters. The objective was to address two research questions, each with a sub-question referencing the challenges faced by Tennessee SME owners during the implementation of innovative disaster preparedness solutions.

The two research questions (RQ) with sub-questions were as follows: *RQ1*: How do Tennessee SME owners implement innovative and technology-driven disaster preparedness solutions to address challenges faced during the preservation of valuable resources? *RQ1a*: How do Tennessee SME owners integrate effective processes to remediate challenging barriers or resource constraints that continue hindering the implementation of technology-driven disaster preparedness solutions? *RQ2*: In what ways do Tennessee SME owners and incident response workforce embrace an innovative technology-driven disaster preparedness solutions-oriented culture within their organizations? *RQ2a*: How do Tennessee SME owners integrate COR theoretical principles and corollaries within organizations to preserve valuable resources by implementing innovative disaster preparedness solutions?

All eight voluntary participants interviewed for this study met the research criteria outlined in the guidelines, recruitment emails, recruitment social media postings, and informed consent forms. Each participant verbally consented to participate in the research study. Transcriptions and code development followed, allowing for the analysis and merging of interrelated codes into sub-themes and themes. Duplicate codes were related and categorized, reducing them from 310 to 42 codes, seven sub-themes, and two themes.

The results were presented based on the themes gathered from the participants who volunteered for this study. **Theme 1** highlighted that SME leaders used lessons learned to overcome preparedness barriers and implement innovative resilience strategies to mitigate disaster risks and ensure business continuity. **Theme 2** revealed that SME workforces aim to foster an innovative preparedness culture by implementing tailored training, prioritizing business continuity (BC), and integrating disaster preparedness solutions.

The data collected demonstrated SME owners, leaders, and stakeholders' disastrous event experiences, unlocking a mindset of implementing technology-driven disaster preparedness measures or integrating solutions within their organizations. Data were collected directly from participants who responded to semi-structured interview questions developed by the qualitative researcher from the study's research questions. A detailed analysis of the findings presented the results aligned with the theoretical framework, which is a basis for the research study. Chapter 4 is finalized with a summary of the discussions.

The purpose of this qualitative exploratory case study was to identify the importance of integrating technology-driven disaster preparedness solutions for SMEs to protect and preserve valuable investment resources (Webb, 2024). This research study adds to the body of knowledge by determining the need to implement innovative and technology-driven disaster preparedness solutions by SME owners, leaders, or stakeholders. Therefore, this exploratory case study addressed the research purpose, problem, and questions to understand the two research questions referencing the perspective of SME owners on implementing technology-driven disaster preparedness solutions.

This research fills a gap in the literature by examining how SME owners implemented innovative preparedness solutions against disruptive events during crises. As a result, the research study focused on SME owners and leaders integrating best practices for revenue growth and business resilience (Webb, 2024). Additionally, the COR theory (Hobfoll, 1989) laid a foundation for a step-by-step process to establish an understanding of this study because of the devastating impacts following disruptive events on SMEs.

Trustworthiness of the Data

Trustworthiness for the qualitative exploratory study was identified in four criteria: credibility, confirmability, dependability, and transferability (Bloomberg, 2022). Trustworthiness criteria promoted thorough data collection and presentation with a critical approach and an accurate explanation to eliminate threats undermining trustworthiness. Trustworthiness was presented from the value of the research study with confidence in the data collected (Jackson, 2024).

The authentic trustworthiness of data collection findings for the research study was to ensure trusted and truthful accounts are presented accountably (Kekeya, 2021). The trustworthiness of the data collected validated the relevance of the qualitative research in Chapter 3 for the research study, with detailed data sources gathered from the semi-structured interviews (H. Karlı et al., 2022; Kekeya, 2021). The collected data were analyzed using thematic analysis to maximize credibility, validity, and reliability to determine integrity. The study's trustworthiness was determined by integrating different measures, such as member checking procedures for the research methodology and design strategies for the information gathered, following an ethical approach for all data findings.

During the exploratory case study, the qualitative researcher conducted semi-structured interviews to collect the data until data saturation was reached by repeatedly interviewing the recruited participants with the same questions (Hennink et al., 2016). According to H. Karlı et al. (2022), data collected from semi-structured interviews must be transcribed, reviewed, and anonymized with pseudonyms to keep participants' information confidential and verified for accuracy by the qualitative researcher. Data were collected from recruited participants, indicating trustworthiness (Kekeya, 2021).

The qualitative researcher identified data credibility from the semi-structured interview findings to identify patterns, whereby transferability replaced the generalizability of the study findings to apply to other settings. This led to the confirmability of the data collected to ensure it did not include my biases or the inclusion of interpretations of outcomes from lessons learned. Therefore, trustworthiness was confirmed with a strong foundation for credibility, transferability, dependability, and confirmability criteria for this exploratory case study.

Confirmability was the initial check the researcher determined for data collection trustworthiness (Bloomberg, 2022). The main goal of confirmability was to ensure the study results did not originate from my biases and interpretations of the data collected. The qualitative researcher was the human instrument; they must have been alerted throughout the research study data collection process. Confirmability was guided to minimize interview time and was reaffirmed from participants' responses by asking questions during the interviews and verbally reiterating their responses.

Confirmability was determined by the research findings, accuracy, and presentation of information without bias by adhering to study expectations and procedures from diverse phases of ongoing processes (Kekeya, 2021). Participants' feelings and thoughts were documented through methods such as journaling, reflexivity, and member checking, establishing credibility by aligning the recruited participants' research with the researcher's perceptions (Bloomberg, 2022). Credibility in the study was identified by thoroughly explaining patterns, themes, and encounters during the data collection process, which can be challenging to understand.

Therefore, the credibility of this study was supported by: (a) Addressing biases with an open attitude through journaling and writing reflective field notes throughout the data collection process. (b) Extending the engagement between the participants and me through repetitive semi-structured interview questionnaires. (c) Integrating realistic procedures to present a thick description. (d) Comparing different sources of data to develop summaries. (e) Ensuring several methods are used to find and present meaningful findings. (f) Presenting discrepancies discovered during the data collection process, including adverse circumstances. (g) Ensuring that my biases did not alter participants' perceptions, which could affect the accuracy of the findings, by using member checking to send transcribed interviews to participants for review. (h) Conducting peer reviews by reaching out to fellow students or coaches to maximize data accuracy from the field notes and journals and to evaluate underlying assumptions, thereby introducing a new approach to viewing and presenting the data.

Therefore, credibility guided the research topic in a reliable, appropriate, and consistent manner by adhering to efficient and accurate procedures and practices to present my experiences and perspectives. This included revalidating all participants' voluntary semi-structured interviews without persuasion. Transcriptions of all interviews were conducted and subsequently forwarded to participants for member checking to confirm, deny, or clarify data collected, fill in missing data, or answer follow-up inquiries to document accurate data findings (Jackson, 2024; Kekeya, 2021).

The qualitative researcher confirmed credibility by continuously verifying and confirming research processes with participants' approval. Overall, the information gathered was refined by separating, grouping, and categorizing until the data findings aligned with the research questions. Credibility and trustworthiness were emphasized using a thorough research process, from data gathering to data analysis and presentation of findings. These elements were essential for ensuring the accuracy, reliability, and validity of the study (Saldaña, 2014).

Data transferability was achieved from the eight participants who provided in-depth and rich data by responding to the semi-structured interview questions, understanding the outcomes of disastrous events, and recognizing the importance of readiness and BC. However, transferability was only established by determining explicit details referencing participants and study content, allowing the reader to judge whether the study applied to their context.

Transferability also refers to the alignment between the study context and other contexts, as perceived by the readers of the study. Transferability in this study was primarily about ensuring readers understand how the study is relatable, valuable, and helpful to others (Bloomberg, 2022). To identify transferability for the research, the study involved significant and singular data focused on a particular circumstance where experiences and activities were relatable and identified.

Transferability was connected to the research topic findings about other studies or experiences to identify data transfer through sound judgment to similar situations (Kekeya, 2021). Bloomberg (2022) defined transferability as the method of relating study findings to determine the study's flexibility, confirming the relative context, and referencing the broader meaning of presenting rich data relevant to the topic. Dependability was identified as the state of certainty that research findings are dependable and can be relied upon, often referring to the consistency of similar studies (Bloomberg, 2022).

The research aimed to be transparent throughout the data collection process to ensure dependability, identifying repetition and consistency in data findings (Jackson, 2024). Credibility was a prerequisite for dependability, as the latter is ineffective without the former (Kekeya, 2021). Dependability was confirmed through IRB approval to conduct research without risks. The IRB application was approved, along with the proposed interview procedure protocol and questions, to ensure that interview questions were open-ended to elicit rich data from participants.

The researcher continuously piloted the interview questions with qualified study participants who met the participation recruitment criteria. The research approach and the findings' dependability relied on consistent and trustworthy data gathering, recording, and exploration. The qualitative researcher verified the information to present and confirm the meanings of data findings through analysis methods by conducting an exploratory case study design to investigate SME owners' implementation of innovative and technology-driven disaster preparedness solutions in Greater Nashville (Jackson, 2024).

The exploratory case study provided detailed and rich data that were dependable and appropriate. The qualitative researcher avoided asking participants leading questions, as they followed the established semi-structured interview questions.

Results

After receiving approval from the Institutional Review Board (IRB-23-24-1208) on June 26, 2024, the data collection process began by recruiting participants in accordance with the recruitment protocol outlined in Chapter 3. Participants were recruited by targeting areas in the Greater Nashville area that had experienced disastrous events within the last two years and sending recruitment emails to all SME owners, leaders, and stakeholders in those areas. Additionally, a recruitment post was published on LinkedIn, seeking eligible voluntary participants for the study.

The qualitative researcher contacted over 134 SME owners and managers via email and social media. Of these, 15 potential participants responded, and semi-structured interviews were scheduled. Overall, eight participants voluntarily participated in the semi-structured interviews. A few participants withdrew before the interviews began, and other interviews were interrupted due to unforeseen circumstances, such as internet connectivity issues caused by hazardous weather or short staffing. Some participants declined to participate without disclosing reasons for not participating in the semi-structured interviews, indicating the challenges of recruiting SME owners for qualitative research.

According to Mishrif and Khan (2023), business owners often do not respond due to organizational shutdowns, time constraints, or busy schedules, which aligns with the qualitative analysis of the eight semi-structured interviews conducted in this study. Similarly, Hennink et al. (2016) and Maluleka and Ross (2024) emphasized the difficulty of recruiting 10 participants for semi-structured interviews, but saturation was achieved when no new data emerged, resulting in new codes, sub-themes or themes.

The number of voluntary participants involved in research can be low across different studies, presenting constraining experiences. For instance, one study recruited only two participants, while another recruited eight, highlighting the challenge of recruiting voluntary participants for diverse research (Barton-Hulsey et al., 2023; Heldring et al., 2024). Similarly, for this study, the qualitative researcher faced the same constraints: Eight eligible participants were recruited, while more than five

SME owners declined participation. Some potential participants stated they needed more disaster preparedness implementation to provide accurate responses to the semi-structured interview questions.

McCourt et al. (2021) conducted a study with 13 participants recruited using convenience, purposive, and snowball sampling methods. However, these methods were not feasible for other studies due to early business closures following disastrous events. For this study, participants were informed of their right to withdraw consent before, during, or after the semi-structured interview, and some chose to withdraw before the interviews began, limiting the number of participants.

Seven SME managers participated in semi-structured interviews for in-depth data collection (Kallmuenzer et al., 2024). Kallmuenzer et al. (2024) noted that existing literature on SME owners' integration of technology-driven planning offers minimal insights. The low number of participants in SME owners' studies highlights the need for future research on technology-driven integrations among SMEs, as this remains a critical area in small business research (Kallmuenzer et al., 2024).

Participants for this study were identified as SME owners or managers who met the following recruitment criteria: they were at least 18 years old, owned or managed an SME in the greater

Nashville area. They had encountered a disastrous event within the last two years. Additionally, voluntary participants included those who had experienced a disastrous event in the past two years or intended to implement technology-driven disaster preparedness solutions within their organizations.

The eight recruited participants for the semi-structured interviews verbally confirmed their consent to participate in the research study voluntarily. Data collection continued until saturation was reached. Each semi-structured interview lasted an average of 45 minutes and was conducted via Zoom video calls with SME owners and managers from different industries in the greater Nashville area from June to September 2024.

The study included eight participants who owned or managed SMEs in the greater Nashville area and had experienced disastrous events, particularly tornadoes, which are predominant in the region. The recruited participants were evenly split, with four females and four males, all of whom had worked in leadership roles between three and 30 years. These participants brought valuable business preparedness and resilience knowledge from their diverse organizational experiences.

Participant P1, a male director of the educational setting's safety and security department, has been in this role for 20 years. P1 confirmed the affordability of implementing technology-driven disaster preparedness solutions.

Participant P2, a female general manager, has been in a senior leadership role at several hotels in the Greater Nashville area for 4 years. P2 confirmed the need for more implementation of technology-driven disaster preparedness solutions due to unaffordability.

Participant P3, a male secretary in a religious entity, has 8 years of experience in the organization. P3 confirmed the unaffordability of implementing technology-driven disaster preparedness solutions within the organization.

Participant P4, a male manager in a hospitality restaurant with over 30 years of experience, also confirmed the lack of technology-driven disaster preparedness solutions due to unaffordability.

Participant P5, a female in the nonprofit sector who has been in a C-suite leadership role for over 8 years, confirmed the unaffordability of implementing technology-driven disaster preparedness solutions.

Participant P6, a female production manager in the construction industry, confirmed the unaffordability of implementing technology-driven or innovative disaster preparedness solutions within the organization.

Participant P7, a male assistant fire chief at one of the fire departments in the Greater Nashville area, has been in the role for over 29 years. P7 confirmed the organization's affordability of technology-driven and innovative disaster preparedness solutions.

Participant P8, a female office administrator in a religious entity in Greater Nashville, has been in the role for 9 years. P8 confirmed the unaffordability of implementing technology-driven disaster preparedness solutions within the organization.

Below is a table presenting the demographics of the participants recruited during the research data collection process.

Data were collected from the eight participants, then transcribed, coded, re-coded, and analyzed using NVivo software. The semi-structured interviews targeted SME owners, leaders, and stakeholders. The collected data were transcribed, coded, and analyzed by grouping and categorizing interrelated coded data into sub-themes and themes. The research study highlighted the importance of implementing effective technology-driven disaster preparedness solutions for SME owners, leaders, and stakeholders in the Greater Nashville to maximize organizational resilience and revenue growth.

Participant Demographics

Table 2. Participant Demographics.

Participant	Gender	Industry	Job role	Years in role	Feasibility of disaster preparedness
P1	Male	Education	Director of Safety Security	20	Affordable
P2	Female	Hospitality (Hotel)	General Manager	4	Unaffordable
P3	Male	Religious Organization	Secretary	8	Unaffordable
P4	Male	Hospitality (Restaurant)	Manager	30	Unaffordable
P5	Female	Nonprofit	Chief Operations Officer	8	Unaffordable
P6	Female	Construction	Production Manager	3	Unaffordable
P7	Male	Fire Department	Assistant Fire Chief	29	Affordable
P8	Female	Religious organization	Office Administrator	9	Unaffordable

Note. The participants' demographics table illustrated the recruited participants' gender, industry of service, job role, years within the specific roles, and feasibility of disaster preparedness standards.

The qualitative researcher conducted semi-structured open-ended interviews to gather data from recruited participants, including SME owners and managers from organizations in the Greater Nashville area. The participants comprised SME owners, leaders, stakeholders, and incident response workforce from businesses that had experienced disastrous events and either implemented technology-driven disaster preparedness solutions or considered integrating readiness procedures. The semi-structured interview questions were designed to reference the research questions and elicit responses from the participants about lessons learned and implementing technology-driven disaster preparedness solutions or readiness measures within organizations.

Data collection included semi-structured interviews to gain in-depth, thick, and rich responses from SME owners and leaders who have implemented disaster preparedness solutions to protect valuable assets and business structures or are considering implementing effective procedures. Investigating the organizational disaster preparedness phenomenon to determine the implementation of technology-driven readiness solutions may add to the body of literature. However, constraints were involved due to the SME owners' and leaders' busy schedules, which limited their availability for the semi-structured interviews. Some scheduled focus group interviews were canceled at the last minute due to unexpected organizational circumstances, such as short staffing, illnesses, and network connectivity disruptions caused by hazardous weather.

To ensure the participants' anonymity and clearly define discussion norms, the researcher explained the purpose of the study and the data collection procedure before obtaining the participants' verbal consent to participate in the research study. The interviewing techniques used for the exploratory case study included semi-structured interviews, which involved investigative methods. The research study addressed general, uncategorized questions while guiding the interviewer and participants through the data-collection process. Participants included SME owners, leaders, and stakeholders from various industries, such as education, nonprofits, hospitality, emergency departments, and restaurants.

Participants had been in specific roles for around four to 30 years, during which they could share lessons learned from past disastrous and disruptive events. Demographic information collected from participants included gender, industry, job role, years in the specific roles, and the feasibility of disaster preparedness within their organizations (Jackson, 2024). Detailed demographic data were not collected to avoid pressuring the voluntary participants or limiting their willingness to participate in the semi-structured interviews. The recordings and transcripts of the interviews were maintained and stored securely throughout the data collection and analysis process. The collected data were stored on an encrypted hard drive in a secure safe for three years.

To identify transferability, the qualitative researcher developed codes and compared them across the transcripts to create sub-themes and themes. This was followed by code analysis using NVivo software to determine the dependability of the data collected. Reviewed and edited transcripts were forwarded to participants for member checking to confirm the credibility of the information and allow participants to add or remove any missed information during the audio or Zoom recordings, including content from field notes.

Data collected were analyzed using open coding, categorizing, and synthesizing findings into themes to determine the interrelation of established codes (Jackson, 2024). The recorded interviews, videos, and audio files were stored securely in a cloud folder and separately on a flash drive in a locked safe to prevent data loss with secure passwords. The qualitative researcher established codes while continuing to analyze existing ones, merging interrelated codes, and categorizing them into sub-themes.

Duplicate codes were deleted, followed by the initiation of sub-themes and themes. The researcher coded and analyzed the transcribed data upon receiving confirmation from participants following member checking of the transcripts, which involved the development of over 310 codes that were reduced to 42 codes, seven sub-themes, and two themes.

Credibility was strengthened through video recording of all interviews and transcription of the recordings. For confidentiality and anonymity, each participant was assigned a numeric code. The codes were merged following patterns identified among the codes to develop themes to minimize the influence of the study's theoretical findings (Jackson, 2024). The qualitative researcher determined the themes and sub-themes using the NVivo software from the codes developed from interview transcripts. The NVivo analysis software was used to identify themes from the coded data as information continued to be assessed for thematic analysis.

The qualitative researcher focused on collecting, transcribing, and analyzing data to condense and make sense of the large amounts of information for practical interpretation (Bloomberg, 2022). Data collected from all eight participants, including four women and four men, were transcribed, coded, and analyzed using NVivo software to identify patterns and themes from the established codes, determining the meaning of the captured findings. The data analysis was an iterative process and was not intended to begin only after information gathering; therefore, the researcher remained vigilant at every phase to identify implications relevant to the study. Data analysis began after collecting the first information (Bloomberg, 2022). The gathered data was analyzed to identify patterns, layers, and information biases or issues to ground or further explain findings.

The study focused on in-depth research addressing data saturation, meaning enough data were collected and no additional themes could be developed, and additional data were unlikely to produce new relevant information or themes (Hennink et al., 2016; Kekeya, 2021). The semi-structured interview questions guided the data collection process, helping to obtain valuable, in-depth, and rich responses from the recruited participants. The collected data were transcribed into Microsoft Word documents using Otter.ai for the interview recordings. Participant names or any indications of names in the transcripts were replaced with pseudonyms and numerical codes to redact organization and individual identities.

Data were collected in large amounts using semi-structured interviews; therefore, early analysis was regulated, minimizing the problem of excessive data by promptly focusing on coding and analysis (Kekeya, 2021). Consistent and constant reviewing and categorizing of coded data were conducted to establish an understanding of the phenomenon being studied. The data collection followed the developed protocol of transcribing the gathered information, coding, analyzing, and categorizing it into themes and sub-themes after determining interrelated codes.

The qualitative data analysis included field notes documented during data gathering, excerpts, and transcripts from semi-structured interviews identified as raw and untouched data

(Bloomberg, 2022). The analysis provided reasons to modify the codes through practical assessment and inferential processes by determining patterns and categorizing codes into sub-themes and theme categories. Data were scrutinized without biases to carefully evaluate findings while interpreting raw data into meaningful insights and unraveling vital information relevant to the study phenomenon.

Qualitative data analysis (QDA) involves reorganizing data findings into structural meanings based on the information gathered (Bloomberg, 2022). Codes were developed from the transcribed data collected from semi-structured interviews, followed by member checking with all participants. The collected data were transformed into compatible codes and then categorized into interrelated sub-themes and themes using NVivo software, which were then securely stored. During the analysis, data were summarized to present discovered themes and patterns. The data analysis process also included diverse structuring of patterns and themes, allowing the identification of meanings in the data findings to address the study's research questions. The analysis of the coded data continued with consistent comparison throughout the study.

The process was not linear but rather a repetitive cycle through numerous phases, looping back and forth and revisiting previous phases to compile and make sense of the data findings, including overlapping one another during data collection (Bloomberg, 2022). A six-phase step approach for qualitative data thematic analysis was both iterative and described as a nonlinear, iterative, and recursive process. This step-by-step analytical approach guided the conclusions of findings from the data collected, ensuring credibility and dependability (Bloomberg, 2022).

A six-phase step approach for qualitative data thematic analysis was iterative, described as a nonlinear, iterative, and recursive process. A step-by-step analytical approach, demonstrating conclusions of findings from the data collected, guides the determination of credibility and dependability (Bloomberg, 2022).

The step-by-step workflow process of the qualitative data analysis involved critical thinking at every stage during coding to ensure the collected data were: a) Revised and investigated, focusing on innovation or technology-driven disaster preparedness while establishing relevant codes; b) Repeatedly assessed to categorize the findings according to interrelationships and related themes and sub-themes; c) Evaluated by including, removing, or minimizing codes in the coding schemes; d) Documented by identifying participant quotations, concluding significant findings from data to information; e) Making sense of findings into knowledge, while adding data collected from journaling, noted summaries, and code descriptions; and f) Interpreted to accurately assess and synthesize analyzed information into a combination of experiences, knowledge, and literature for the study (Bloomberg, 2022).

The QDA minimized the coded data by categorizing related codes into sub-themes and themes into assessed information, removing redundant and repetitive data while establishing thematic categories (Bloomberg, 2022). Data analysis was time-consuming, whereby the qualitative researcher integrated several phases of procedures with the expectation that it would lead to an iterative process that continued to introduce new interpretations.

RQ1

How do Tennessee SME owners implement innovative and technology-driven disaster preparedness solutions to address challenges while preserving valuable resources?

RQ1a

How do Tennessee SME owners integrate effective processes to remediate challenging barriers or resource constraints that hinder the implementation of technology-driven disaster preparedness solutions?

The response to RQ1 and RQ1a involved 16 codes, four sub-themes, and one theme. The four sub-themes were analyzed from 16 codes, including (a) lessons learned from disastrous events, (b) barriers and constraints hindering disaster preparedness implementation, (c) innovative integration of disaster preparedness solutions to promote business resilience, and (d) impacts emanating from disastrous events affecting BC. Conversely, the four categories were minimized into Theme One: SME owners, leaders, and stakeholders, understanding from lessons learned the importance of mitigating disaster preparedness barriers and constraints by investing in business resilience and remediating disaster risk through BC and DR.

Theme 1. SME Owners, Leaders, and Stakeholders Understanding From Lessons Learned the Importance of Mitigating Disaster Preparedness Barriers and Constraints by Investing in Business Resilience and Remediating Disaster Risk Through BC and DR. Theme 1 entailed four sub-themes and numerous codes. The first sub-theme to conclude with Theme 1 explained how DR and BC planning reduced disaster risk and invested in business resilience, thereby addressing barriers and constraints to incorporate disaster preparedness strategies through SME owners' comprehension of lessons learned (see Table 2 for Theme 1 coding information).

Theme 1 SME Owners' Lessons Learned to Develop Mitigatory Strategies

Table 3. Theme 1 SME Owners' Lessons Learned to Develop Mitigatory Strategies.

Theme	Sub-themes	Codes
From lessons learned, SME owners and leaders understanding of the importance to implement technology-driven disaster preparedness solutions against barriers and constraints; this can be mitigated by investing in business resilience, remediating disaster risk, and integrating BC and DR.	Lessons learned from disastrous experiences	Procedures from lessons learned Disaster preparedness strategies implementation from lessons learned. Maximizing and acquiring necessary readiness resources Disastrous events influence on SME owners' and leaders' perception Accurate documentation of disastrous events as lessons learned Lesson learned from tornado and flooding disastrous events
	Barriers and constraints hindering the implementation of technology-driven disaster preparedness solutions.	SME owners not considering disaster preparedness solutions as compelling Disaster preparedness solutions operated in an "ad hoc reaction posture."

Theme	Sub-themes	Codes
		Leadership decision-making delays, which affect the implementation of disaster preparedness solutions
		Lack of innovative and technology-driven preparedness solutions as an existing gap
		Lack of disaster preparedness training, although considered a necessity
		Financial limitations to invest in technology-driven disaster preparedness solutions
		Leadership challenges due to the lack of competency in disaster preparedness and BC planning
	Integration of innovative technology-driven solutions to promote business resilience	Implementing innovative mitigatory strategies with artificial intelligence (AI) driven tools, robotics, and drones
		Use of innovative and technology-driven emergency preparedness products

Theme	Sub-themes	Codes
	Disastrous Events Impacting BC	Disastrous events causing destruction and disrupting business operations
		Communication disruptions following a disastrous event affecting BC, including a displaced workforce.

Note. Table 3 illustrated Theme 1 - SME owners' and leaders' understanding of lessons learned on mitigating disaster preparedness barriers and constraints by investing in business resilience and remediating disaster risk through BC and DR strategies.

Participants P2, P3, P4, P5, P6, and P8 all confirmed a need for more financial resources to invest in implementing technology-driven disaster preparedness solutions within organizations. According to P3, "minimally to none, really anything might be considered an event is handled pretty much in a responsive manner." Additionally, P3 continued by stating, "Our phone system depends on our electricity… not just for the church system but also to communicate with the congregation."

As P3 reflected, P2, P4, P5, P6, and P8 explained how the lack of leadership and timely decision-making affects BC during or following a disastrous event. This was highlighted by P3, who stated, "I am not sure what the priority is in terms of disaster preparedness or where our governing body has placed." P4 added by stating what the workforce prepares on what procedures to follow when a disaster occurs; the most significant thing is to make sure whoever is in the store knows how to deal with situations that come up because all the cell phone towers are clogged up. Only marginal contact with your crew exists during a disastrous event; therefore, leadership must ensure the workforce understands and follows everything discussed regarding their safety.

P4 reaffirmed, "When it goes down ... with technology, there are no phone calls will solve it all or no internet access will answer all your questions because you want to make sure whoever is taking care of where you have lived."

P4 concluded by stating, "There is no weather radio; however, we do have a television here we have hooked to our Wi-Fi, so ... if anything is going on, we find ways out." P4 added, "We have a silent alarm for burglary scenarios that could be hit. However, in situations middle of or after a tornado, the police officers will be there anyway." In contrast, P7, like all other participants, explained falling short a couple of times due to a lack of effective disaster preparedness solutions and having learned through the experiences, leading to better collaborative efforts with surrounding agencies.

Conversely, P5 iterated on implementing technology-driven disaster preparedness solutions, "being honest, I do not think this is a level conversation we have had in our organization, and I do not want to jump too far ahead." P5 continued to explain what disaster preparedness solutions were implemented for BC following the COVID-19 pandemic, "providing hands-on sanitizer for the workforce … administering screens to ensure temperatures were checked… setting up tents outside to continue business operations, and avoiding working in tight spaces." P5 added, "the organization's focus was shifted from doing job readiness classes and fighting for employment to helping people navigate COVID money out there and helping with unemployment because there were jobs… to serve people in need." In contrast to other participants for BC, P5 explained, we did use emails more … especially for the technical side, which can be difficult because we are an in-person organization, and many times, our participants might not have phones and things like that, so the way for them to access us is coming on-site.

Like P2, P5 confirmed how the organization's leadership continues discussions on the intention to implement disaster preparedness solutions. P5 indicated integration intentions by stating, "We did have to look at communication, though I would say better use of technology, we still have not expanded, and we are not doing remote work … because our work is people-facing." Disastrous events affect business revenue growth, employment, and organizational resilience if SME owners do not implement technology-driven disaster preparedness solutions and are not concurred by all participants.

Details on BC planning were briefly discussed by P1, P4, P5, and P7, whereby P5 best exemplified it by stating, "The biggest thing is just being able to pivot and not being stuck in like what you are used to doing." P5 added,

I know disasters could be multiple things or whatnot. However, I think… being able to talk to your key stakeholders … and different companies that we partnered with were like, what are you guys doing, what are you hearing, and so we communicated with other organizations.

Participants P1, P5, and P7 all agreed on the importance of effectively communicating with stakeholders to discuss the way forward following a disastrous event to promote collaborative efforts. On the financial aspect, P5 confirmed, some nonprofits … got the paycheck protection program (PPP) loans - COVID money that businesses got, but some other nonprofit partners, even for our social enterprises, gave us additional money that they had received so we could distribute it to other nonprofit organizations.

P5 elaborated on leadership's intentions to implement disaster-prepared solutions, "insurance policies … to cover cyberattacks, fraud, scams … so that we can recover while … we work on upgrading our technology."

Like all other participants, P5 explained that "funding and time" are essential for implementing technology-driven disaster preparedness solutions in organizations. In contrast to the other participants recruited, P6's response to the implementation of technology-driven disaster preparedness was, "I cannot reply as we do not have anything like this in place," P6 reaffirmed briefly, "again, we are a small company, and for disaster preparedness, we just know when to go inside or to the cellar." In contrast, P7 elaborated on how the greater Nashville area is prone to disasters by stating, "In this part of the United States, we are very susceptible to flooding."

Similarly, all participants except P6 agreed as P7 emphasized the lessons learned by stating, "So what we have learned from previous disastrous events is we had not paid attention to those floodplains because if we had paid attention to those floodplains, we would have enforced codes effectively." Conversely, P7 added, "we allowed things to be built in areas … that was not going to hold up in a situation like that, and when it happened, it created major disruption for our department and surrounding departments." In addition, P7 elaborated, "from lessons learned and previous lack of disaster preparedness strategies to handle large scale natural disasters."

Participants P2, P4, P7, and P8 concurred on how they are prone to experiencing disastrous impacts from tornadoes but do not deal with hurricanes and large-scale natural events. This was discussed as an impactful lesson learned, reported by most participants, identifying all SME owners, leaders, stakeholders, and incident response teams need to transform their thinking and communication to get everybody on the same page.

To avoid disaster response delays, P7 explained, "Instead of independent communication centers … we have one communication center that handles all of the dispatching and call-taking information for all 911 organizations, fire departments, emergency medical services (EMS), and police." P7 continued explaining the importance of implementing effective disaster preparedness solutions introduced to the workforce, "by doing that, we realized we had to increase our resources to handle those situations … so we had to create Swiftwater teams and dive teams … to handle flash flooding and natural disaster-type situations." Part of the lesson learned from the 100-year flood and its destruction, as P7 discussed, was, "structures were destroyed … so we had to create further boundaries for flood plain areas … to mitigate when it does happen again."

Although disaster preparedness implementation has been discussed by all participants, except for P6, they all concurred with uncertainty about the unfortunate limitations of financial resources affecting the integration of readiness measures, taking almost 20 to 30 years. The effects of the financial limitations that all other participants reported were also confirmed by P7 when he explained, "If there is any big constraint ... emergency services, it is always going to be financial, which is our biggest constraint hindering the implementation of any type of disaster preparedness solution."

Correspondingly, technology-driven solutions integrated by the organization for prompt response were confirmed by P7 as "the dispatch information comes out and is sent to those computers, personnel can get in those trucks and start responding ... to 911 calls." Additionally, reconstruction to mitigate disaster risk was confirmed by P8, who explained, "I think the lesson learned is ... rebuilding to ... make sure access to safe spaces ... and adding those gel pack bags for any potential flooding." P8 added, "We do have a complete fire alarm system ... a mic alarm system if we needed to get on and make announcements which could be heard throughout the building." As reported by all other participants, P8 concluded, "I would say the technology barriers would be cost-related," which all other participants continued to communicate, except for P6.

RQ2

In what ways do Tennessee SME owners and incident response workforce embrace an innovative technology-driven disaster preparedness solutions-oriented culture within their organizations?

RQ2a

How do Tennessee SME owners integrate COR theoretical principles and corollaries within organizations to preserve valuable resources by implementing innovative disaster preparedness solutions?

The response to RQ2 and RQ2a included 15 codes, three sub-themes, and one theme. The three sub-themes developed from the 15 codes included (a) implementation of innovatively tailored preparedness training, (b) BC prioritization following a disastrous event, and (c) processes promoting the integration of disaster preparedness solutions. Subsequently, the three categories were minimized into Theme 2: Fostering innovative disaster preparedness solutions as a culture adhering to integrating tailored training and prioritizing BC should be understood by the SME workforce following recommended guidance and standards from the COR theory.

Theme 2. Fostering Innovative Disaster Preparedness Solutions As a Culture Adhering to Integrating Tailored Training And Prioritizing BC Should Be Understood by The SME Workforce

Theme 2 listed three sub-themes and 15 codes. The first sub-theme listed under the theme involved understanding the SME workforce's prioritization to integrate an innovative preparedness culture, tailored disaster preparedness training, BC prioritization, and processes and standards leading to the integration of disaster preparedness solutions.

Theme 2 SME Workforces' Fostering of A Preparedness Culture

Table 4. Theme 2 SME Workforces' Fostering of a Preparedness Culture.

Theme	Sub-Themes	Codes
Fostering innovative disaster preparedness solutions as a culture adhering to integrating tailored training and prioritizing BC and should be understood by the SME workforce.	Implementing innovatively tailored preparedness training	Integrating emergent and innovative strategic preparedness operation plans
		Emergency management training to promote disaster preparedness posture
		Technology-driven disaster preparedness training
		Accessible lifesaving, innovatively tailored training
		Annual disaster preparedness training compliance
		Business owners' contribution to disaster preparedness training programs
		Preparedness training against chemicals
		SME disaster preparedness training solutions on a limited scale

Theme	Sub-Themes	Codes
	BC prioritization following a disastrous event	Disaster preparedness procedures following a disruptive events
		Leaderships' flexible and prompt decisions for effective BC
	Preparedness procedures promoting the integration of disaster preparedness training solutions	Essential BC collaborative efforts
		Financial access to fund and promote BC after a disastrous event
		Leveraging the integration of disaster preparedness solutions
		Communication through miscellaneous channels
		Technology-driven disaster preparedness solutions integrated with effective communication

Note. Table 4 illustrates Theme 2 - SME workforces' understanding of the importance of adopting innovative and technology-driven disaster preparedness-tailored training culture prioritizing BC and DR strategies.

Participant P1 was the first to discuss the integration of disaster preparedness-tailored training culture within the organization to promote business readiness and resilience. P1 explained that following a disastrous event, "I develop emergency operation plans for schools and the district emergency operation plan in support of schools as they return to normal." P1 added, "Resources added to the training include transportation facilities, safety, security, and nutrition services." Conversely, P1 confirmed, "When it comes to emergency management ... we do CPR and AED training; we provide the supplies for stop bleed kits, backpacks, and each of the classrooms for medical and other types of tools."

P1 and P3 confirmed the integration of CPR classes every couple of years with AED machines. As confirmed by P1, AED training leads to "having AEDs spread throughout the school ... and so it is just one of the things we do regarding preparedness." P1 echoed P3's sentiments by stating, "I will tell you the state requires school districts to have an emergency operations plan in the district to have an overall district plan ... each school must do a security assessment with the principal and their local law enforcement."

Additionally, P1 concluded by stating, "Doors are required to be secure ... many schools have visitor management processes, and school resource officer (SRO) programs ... have a safety and security department internally... coordinated along with our office of Emergency Management." P1 and P3 explained the presence of First Aid kits around the facility.

Participant P1 elaborated on the importance of safety like P2, P3, P4, P5, P7, and P8 by stating, "The safety and security department … gives guidance and framework to … conduct drills either with … local law enforcement officers." Subsequently, P1 added, " … a fire drill through which students and staff are supposed to diversify those drills, and then do an after-action report on the deficiency so they can be better next time." One of the factors repeated by P1 resonated with all participants was, "communication, communication, communication is always the issue, the ability to access information through data terminals, and cars … to share information from different strike teams." Additionally, to support technology-driven solutions, P1 and P7 confirmed that one of their more effective communication methods was to use platforms like Navigate 360 to document emergency plans, drills, and training programs.

Subsequently, P1 discussed virtual training capabilities: "We take advantage of online training for different people who work on our emergency plans." Workforce training was confirmed as advantageous by P1, stating, "We have different locking mechanisms throughout the school district … which shows us who, where, and when an individual enters the building, and we train our people on territorial reinforcement techniques."

Training courses were funded by FEMA, which most SME owners should be made aware of, as confirmed by P1 and P7. P1 added, "Each school principal was asked to partake in courses such as IS-100 and IS-700 through FEMA's Emergency Management Institute (EMI), along with other staff." P1 explained, "A lot goes into a layered approach ... working closely with our office of emergency management ... we are also involved in the overall County's emergency plan, and they are involved in ours." P2 elaborated that local firefighters offered free training, saying, "It is a free scheduling service with the firefighters; we are lucky enough we can get service from the area." P2 also mentioned that the firefighters work collaboratively with the security team.

The organizations promoted annual compliance training to empower the workforce, as confirmed by P1, P2, and P7, whereby all other participants denied any form of disaster preparedness training integration within their organization. P2 emphasized, "We have refresher courses and videos for our employees ... for the drills, we do them every end of the quarter." Prior to attending the annual compliance training courses, emails are sent as reminders to the workforce, as confirmed by participants P1, P2, and P7.

Participant P2 explained how the videos help guide the workforce to best prepare for disastrous events by stating, "...having all those videos and refresher courses, they helped us like to mitigate these risks that could cause these disasters." P1 added, "Everybody wants to be able to protect children the best they can, so training is part of it, and we have professionals here, so they understand they got to get trained."

The advantages of integrating training effectively were clarified by participant P1, stating, " … we have another layer, as I mentioned about the elementary school ambassador program." P1 continued, " … a layperson, we provide training to … ensure exterior doors are secure, hall monitoring, doing sweeps of parking lots in the perimeter, working with the school emergency plan, and … to respond to incidents on campus."

An example emphasized by P2 was that the recent outage from CrowdStrike affected the use of the Microsoft network; the emergency department team ensured the workforce was informed on time. Training was another factor highlighted by P2 to ensure the workforce is proficient in using technological devices and phones before they are provided, although working remotely persisted as a challenge. P2 integrating AI-focused training would promote expedited information sharing.

In contrast, P3 confirmed the lack of training for technology-driven disaster preparedness. Therefore, P3 elaborated that when disastrous circumstances occurred, "trees were down, we had no electricity… the impact on our disaster awareness would be how to notify the congregation there is a situation here … would be our big question." P3 added, "Since our phone system is dependent on our electricity, it would have to be something that could be transferred to or integrated with people's cell phones, not just the church system."

Similarly, this experience was shared by most participants, P2, P3, P4, P5, P6, and P8, who expressed the lack of financial resources to implement technology-driven disaster preparedness solutions within the organizations, thereby affecting BC in disastrous events. P4 elaborated on how impacts differ, "like in 1998, I was at the store when the tornado went down … and we did not even lose power for 24 hours … and we were back up and running the next day."

P4 explained, "You never know until it happens," referring to a disastrous event. P4 confirmed how he trains his workforce by stating, "I tell my crew if anything is out of the ordinary, like the tornado we just got hit with, right through this path in December, it is our safety before anything else. We have got a walk-in cooler bolted down."

P4 continued to reaffirm that "we do not go through a set training … to keep costs down… when it goes down, technology does not have a factor in it because there is no set routine for a building just blowing away or the roads shut down".

Similarly, participants P3 and P4 elaborated on the importance of the workforce's safety first above anything else in disastrous event circumstances, which all other participants also expressed. P4 continued to reaffirm, "I have got superstitious about leaving the building when there is certain weather, when they call for certain things to happen day, if the weather says, hey, it is going to happen, we just do not know then." According to P4, "the worst case scenario is when it does happen, all store owners and everything we all tried to get to wherever we can help out the fastest course a lot of time, by the time the area is in gridlock. You cannot get in or out."

Due to the lack of training integrated within the organization, P4 explained,

> This is a family-owned business, and many days on hold affect everybody's income, so we need to communicate with each other about our next steps. We all send regular messages back and forth. This tells the workforce the best way to handle those scenarios, which goes for whoever is in charge. The number two, number three and high school kids working for you at night need to know all those tips as well.

On BC, P5 clarified, "Our information technology (IT) coworker left but ensured all the organizational data were backed up on the drive." P5 added, "The challenge is not all systems collaborate ... the software does not necessarily merge, so having different software for different things can be challenging."

As participants P3, P4, P6, and P8 confirmed, P5 added, "We do not attend training often," referring to disaster preparedness training; "we need to implement training, and I think there are some resources out there, but they have not been at the forefront."

Subsequently, P5 elaborated, "The organization prides itself on being innovative; we develop programs … like any aspect of the program, so when COVID came, we were like, okay, what can we do." For business continuity, P5 explained, "Our housing director took pieces of wood and plexiglass and built the plastic dividers … our disinfecting business … we already had some of the disinfecting supplies … for the disinfecting service."

P5 stressed the importance of disaster preparedness strategies by stating, "Continuing to exercise the muscle so when we get in these crises, you are not so used to being boxed in." For business continuity, P5 added, "In case of a tornado, we will have someone outside letting people get the message out we have to shut down" as a recovery response.

Contrarywise, P5, like P1 and P7, confirmed having integrated a layered approach in different vital programs. P5 elaborated on organizational endeavors to figure out what each workforce team plays when a disastrous event occurs, which could mean temporarily pivoting the mission duties. Furthermore, in times of disastrous events, P5 elaborated on the organization's efforts to determine the role of each workforce team during a disastrous event, which might involve temporarily adjusting mission duties. In times of disastrous events, P5 continued to emphasize the importance of leadership team management skills to ensure the workforce remains innovative in managing disruptive situations.

P5 highlighted the challenge of low funding resources experienced by the organization to invest in training programs, stating, "A lot of the funding usually comes from donors, and things like might want to spend on programs." The funding identified by P5 can be considered as grants or donations from specific donors, making it possible to invest in training programs.

Mitigatory solutions were implemented, as confirmed by P5, by storing critical data on the drive, thereby providing the ability to access files remotely, especially during the COVID-19 pandemic. During plans to integrate preparedness training, P5 expressed ongoing discussions to integrate insurance policies as a disaster preparedness mitigatory solution was currently in an exploratory phase among the leadership team, an intentional conversation. Additional preparedness measures for P5 discussed included backing up data on a drive to minimize the overwhelming circumstances of paper storage within the organization.

All participants except P6 agreed on the importance of transparency and flexibility in using available resources to respond to a disastrous event with a solution-oriented perspective. In contrast, P6 did not explain any form of approach. To foster BC within the organization, P5 indicated, "We use Google as the organizational Gmail hub … as far as being able to access our documents remotely." Another platform implemented by the participant, like P5, to store customer data and donor information was Salesforce, in addition to different software systems for different purposes.

Training and BC integration, as explained by P7, allowed the workforce to collaborate and exchange tools with other groups for expedited response, thereby reducing the response times required for specific emergencies or areas within the scope of disastrous events. Similar to P1, P7 added that disaster preparedness training minimized response and call-taking times to nearly zero, which is critical for both EMS calls and fire emergencies competing against the clock. An effectively trained workforce led to collaborative efforts with other networks and agencies, as specified by P7. All participants, except P6, confirmed that collaborative efforts are vital to restoring BC and DR following a disastrous event, with support from other agencies or resources, as P7 indicated.

Disaster preparedness training for the workforce was highlighted to introduce challenges, as confirmed by P7, due to the continued evolving solutions, "the fact that training continues to evolve as time goes on by introducing better solutions that are being developed." With the exception of P7 from all participants, the concern of learning to use certain types of computer systems and different websites and then turning around and having all newly learned technological skills changed. Additionally, P7 expressed the worry of continuing training and ensuring the workforce constantly evolves with innovative technology and information improvements.

Most of the training, as previously identified for emergency response preparedness, goes through government agencies like FEMA grants, as confirmed by P7. Many business leaders are not aware of these grants, which provide opportunities for organizations to promote effective disaster preparedness training programs and courses covered by the government. Other grants also exist providing emergency service training accessible for SME owners to promote readiness training. When the workforce is trained efficiently, all employees work together under one roof, fostering a team spirit.

This unified approach, as confirmed by P1 and P7, contributes to long-term resilience against disruptive events within the organization. Participants P1 and P7 added that technology-driven disaster preparedness strategies have not yet been fully utilized. Conversely, P2, P3, P4, P5, P6, and P8 have not invested in readiness solutions. P7 added, it is like having a football team, and you practice them every day, but they never have a chance to go play a game … so they do not really know how good they are because all they have to do is practice with each other.

P7 elaborated on some examples of technology-driven preparedness equipment, including drones and thermal imaging cameras. Drones are used for aerial imaging, surveillance, mapping, and delivering supplies, while thermal imaging cameras are utilized for detecting heat signatures, identifying hazards, and locating individuals in low-visibility conditions. Both tools are essential for communication, situational awareness, and enhancing disaster response efforts. On the other hand, P8 mentioned constructing a "dug-in basement" as a safe space during disasters. However, investment in other disaster preparedness measures was prevalent than readiness training. P8 acknowledged that the lack of readiness training stems from insufficient funding, a challenge shared by most other participants.

Evaluation of the Findings

The research design for this study was an exploratory case study illustrating the need for implementing innovative and technology-driven disaster preparedness solutions by Tennessee SME owners. The findings from the data collected were used to explore the problem SME owners continue facing in their endeavors to integrate effective disaster preparedness solutions to preserve SME owners' valuable investments and resources, guided by the COR theory (Hobfoll, 1989). The case study data collection findings indicated consistent similarities, differences, and contributions in the literature review of how SME owners have been devastatingly impacted by disastrous events, leading to early business closure due to business disruption, mainly due to a lack of technology-driven disaster preparedness solutions integration (Hoerold et al., 2021; J. Ha et al., 2022; T. Oyama et al., 2021; Tosun & Bostan, 2021).

Liang et al. (2023) discussed data findings were consistent, whereby SMEs are reported as vulnerable upon facing a disastrous event, as over 40–60 percent never reopened after a disruptive event, as seen during the 2017 Hurricane Harvey in impacted communities. Small businesses should estimate the expected length of recovery and prepare a BC plan accordingly, evaluating the vulnerability and resilience needed to preserve valuable resources.

Liang et al. (2023) also confirmed that businesses investing in resilience and recovery efforts could minimize their mean and median recovery times by 57 percent and 8.5 percent, respectively. Therefore, SME owners' ability to invest in preparedness solutions guided organizations to withstand disasters and recover quickly from disruptive events, especially in the business environment. The study findings will be directly applicable to SME owners, managers, and stakeholders, providing practical strategies for enhancing disaster preparedness and resilience. Additionally, policymakers and disaster response owners can integrate these insightful findings to develop targeted programs and interventions that address the specific needs and challenges faced by SME owners and managers in disaster-prone regions.

Conversely, disastrous events have led to inadequate recovery procedures among different economic groups, with SMEs being particularly affected (Alisjahbana et al., 2022). In the context of earthquake recovery and its consequences, SMEs should establish an agent-based financial model for recovery assistance. Case studies on the experiences encountered by SMEs following disruptive events provide assessments that enable other small businesses to develop mitigatory strategies, thereby reducing disparities and inequities in recovery.

Financial resources are a significant factor, as indicated in this study, making it essential to rebuild destroyed businesses. The agent-based model mitigates the gap created by the lack of financial resources by incorporating diverse financial sources supported by government agencies:

(a) Disaster risk insurance,

(b) FEMA,

(c) SBA,

(d) Community Development Block Grants for Disaster Recovery (CDBG-DR),

(e) Private banks,

(f) Non-Governmental organizations (NGOs), and

(g) Business savings. According to Alisjahbana et al. (2022), SBA loans cover costs by providing financial resources that need to be fully recovered by business insurance or structural repairs.

Geographical and Demographic Limitations

Precision Geographical Limitations

The study presented SME owners and managers in the greater Nashville area and limited its generalization to other regions or contexts. This meant the findings were specific to this geographical area and may not fully apply to SME owners in other cities or countries. The focus on Tennessee SMEs is particularly relevant due to the unique disaster risks and economic context of the region. Tennessee, and the greater Nashville area specifically, has experienced a variety of natural and man-made disasters in recent years, including floods, tornadoes, and significant infrastructure failures (Tennessee Emergency Management Agency, 2021).

These events have highlighted the vulnerabilities of SMEs, which form a crucial part of the local economy. Additionally, Tennessee's diverse economic landscape, which includes industries such as manufacturing, healthcare, and technology, provides a rich context for examining the implementation of disaster preparedness solutions. By focusing on SMEs in this specific geographic area, the study aims to generate insights that are highly relevant to the local context while also offering broader implications for similar regions facing comparable risks and challenges (Smith & Anderson, 2020).

Sample Size

With eight participants, the sample size was small. In qualitative research, small sample sizes are often acceptable because this is a common issue in qualitative studies, where depth of insight is prioritized over breadth (Bloomberg, 2022; Creswell, 2013). By employing semi-structured interviews and thematic analysis, the methodology enabled an in-depth examination of the interview questions by capturing detailed insights from SME owners and managers (Creswell, 2013).

This sample size was consistent with qualitative research standards, which often recommend smaller, focused samples to provide in-depth insights. The chosen sample size of eight participants was justified by the principle of data saturation, which was reached when no new information or themes were observed in the data (Guest et al., 2006; Hennink et al., 2016). This guided the researcher to arrive at meaning and code saturation (Hennink et al., 2017).

This was evident during the data collection process when no new data or codes emerged from transcripts. This also ensured that the constructs were thoroughly discussed, modified, and confirmed by the researcher, addressing the literature gaps with the provision of a comprehensive understanding of the implementation strategies and challenges faced by Tennessee SME owners (Kekeya, 2021).

Methodological Limitations

Given the research's focus on an in-depth exploration of factors and strategies in disaster preparedness and the decision to use a qualitative research methodology, there are implied limitations in the generalizability of the findings. The results will not be applicable to all areas subjected to natural disasters, but only to SMEs with specific characteristics and in certain locations. Expanding on the limitations related to participant recruitment is essential to understand how these limitations might have affected the generalizability of the findings.

The study's sample size might have been small, and participants could have been from a specific demographic or geographic area, such as SME owners in the greater Nashville area of Tennessee. This means the findings might not be representative of all SME owners in different regions or industries. A larger and more diverse sample would have enhanced the generalizability of the results to a broader population (Bloomberg, 2022; Mohajan, 2018).

Since the study relied on qualitative methods, such as interviews, it was not easy to apply statistical analysis or generalize findings quantitatively. Qualitative research typically focuses more on exploring experiences, patterns, and meanings than numerical data or broad statistical trends. Participants may have provided socially desirable responses or omitted specific details, leading to potential inaccuracies in the data.

Respondent bias is common in interviews where participants want to present themselves or their businesses favorably. Despite efforts to maintain objectivity, the researcher's beliefs or perspectives could still influence the interpretation of the data. It is a common concern in qualitative research, where the researcher is actively involved in data collection and interpretation. To minimize researcher bias, the researcher annotated the data extensively to stay close to the participants' stated meanings.

Trustworthiness and Validity

The study's trustworthiness was presented in the research. Trustworthiness was critical in qualitative research to ensure credible and reliable findings. Four criteria were used to assess this:

1. **Credibility:** This refers to the accuracy and authenticity of the findings. It was ensured by identifying patterns in the data from the semi-structured interviews and by using transferability instead of generalizability (i.e., applying findings to similar contexts rather than assuming they apply universally).

2. **Confirmability:** This criterion addresses the need for the research findings to be free of my biases or personal interpretations. The qualitative researcher sought to ensure the results were based on the participants'

experiences, not on my assumptions. Confirmability was strengthened by minimizing the interview time and keeping data collection transparent and systematic.

3. **Dependability:** The study's dependability was established by ensuring transparency in the data collection process, providing evidence of consistency in findings, and having the process reviewed and approved by an Institutional Review Board (IRB). Dependability was also reinforced by using structured interview questions designed to extract rich, in-depth responses.

4. **Transferability:** This refers to the extent to which findings can be applied to other contexts. The qualitative researcher aimed to document the lessons learned from the Nashville SME owners, which could be exemplified in similar business settings, particularly in terms of BC and DR for disaster preparedness. The in-depth interviews with the 8 participants provided rich data that could potentially inform broader applications, even if they are geographically or contextually different.

While there were limitations in terms of sample size, geographic scope, and methodological constraints (such as the inability to generalize or quantify findings), the qualitative researcher worked to ensure the trustworthiness of the data through credibility, confirmability, dependability, and transferability. These steps helped enhance the validity and relevance of the research, even though the findings are not universally applicable. The research questions evaluation of findings presented assessments of data collection and research findings.

Research Findings

RQ1.

How do Tennessee SME Owners Implement Innovative And Technology-Driven Disaster Preparedness Solutions to Address Challenges Faced During The Preservation of Valuable Resources?

RQ1a.

How do Tennessee SME Owners Integrate Effective Processes to Remediate Challenging Barriers or Resource Constraints That Continue Hindering The Implementation of Technology-Driven Disaster Preparedness Solutions?

For Theme 1, the findings indicated SME owners, leaders, and stakeholders understood from lessons learned the importance of mitigating disaster preparedness barriers and constraints by investing in business resilience and remediating disaster risk through BC and DR. This assessment was consistent with the data collected from all recruited participants and the literature review emphasizing on the importance of integrating effective technology-driven disaster preparedness solutions. The lack of financial resources posed obstacles whereby SME owners are hindered from the integration of efficient policies and technology-driven disaster preparedness solutions (Sarmiento et al., 2019; Varga-Florez et al., 2020).

Another conclusion consistent with the data findings was how SME owners incorporated rainy day fund (RDF) frameworks to minimize financial stress or business closure following a disastrous impact (J. Ha et al., 2022; Lee & Chen, 2021; Sarmiento et al., 2019). Conversely, for all participants interviewed using semi-structured interviews, only P1 and P7 confirmed the affordability of investing in readiness measures, which included robust measures, consistent preparedness training, BC planning, and DR.

Subsequently, the adoption of policies and frameworks by SME owners promoted the implementation of technology-driven and innovative disaster preparedness solutions and integration of readiness training, which leveraged a strong business resilient culture and enabled effective responses against disruptive events (Q. S. A. Ali et al., 2023; Sarmiento et al., 2019). P5 confirmed the existence of a rainy day fund (RDF) framework within their organization, which was utilized during the COVID-19 pandemic.

P5 emphasized the importance of discussing with key stakeholders to call different companies partnering with the organization to discuss the approach and what they knew about the disastrous event impacts. Additional financial support was obtained from government entities, such as the regular PPP loans, including support from nonprofit partners and social enterprises, which donated additional funds they had also received. The words of P5 reflected what all other participants shared on the competency and promptness of the leadership team's decision-making direction in times of disastrous events for the safety of the workforce.

Participant P5's lesson learned was demonstrated by giving credit to the leadership team and Chief Executive Officer (CEO) for effectively managing the organization during and after the COVID-19 pandemic. This involved iterating on their strategies to adapt to the changing circumstances and ensuring the organization's continued resilience and success. P5 added by stating, I do not know how she did it because navigating COVID was hard, but when I tell you she did it the best, she could do a good job, so I think you know it really has a trusted team to make the hard decisions.

Conversely, a humanistic approach to qualitative data collection was best supported by creating a humanistic story with the data. The research findings reference the COR theoretical framework identified in Chapter 2 of the study and the literature review of the research project. In addition, the findings presented the need to reflect only the data answering the study's research questions and reported in line with the individual research questions.

Among the participants, two out of eight demonstrated confidence in technology-driven disaster preparedness against disruptive events, while the other six confirmed the lack of financial resources to invest in innovative readiness solutions. For instance, P2, P3, P4, P5, P6, and P8 all concurred "minimally to none, really anything might be considered as an event is handled pretty much in a responsive manner."

RQ2.

In What Ways Do Tennessee SME Owners And Incident Response Workforce Embrace An Innovative Technology-Driven Disaster Preparedness Solutions-Oriented Culture Within Their Organizations? *RQ2a.* How do Tennessee SME Owners Best Integrate The COR Theoretical Principles and Corollaries Within Organizations to Preserve Valuable Resources by Implementing Innovative Disaster Preparedness Solutions?

For **Theme 2**, the findings denoted SME workforce understanding of fostering an innovative disaster preparedness culture by adhering to integrated, tailored training and prioritizing BC. This conclusion was consistent with the literature, whereby disastrous impacts affect BC by destroying business structures, flow of communication, medical services, and the displacement of employees (Asgary et al., 2020; Green, 2023; Gwon et al., 2022; Leary et al., 2023; Saad et al., 2021; Sarmiento et al., 2019).

Conversely, a well-trained incident response workforce exemplifies strong disaster preparedness skills through the training acquired, thereby responding to disruptive events effectively and ensuring the stability for BC (Alexander et al., 2023; Leary et al., 2023; Shweta et al., 2022; T. Oyama et al., 2021). However, only P1, P2, and P7 confirmed the presence of effective disaster preparedness training, whereby an effective readiness response towards disastrous events exists within the organization, ensuring an effective readiness response to disastrous events.

Data collection on disaster preparedness training from P3, P4, P5, P6, and P8 was consistent with the literature reviewed, which confirmed the lack of SME owners' lack of investment in technology-driven readiness training often led to inaccurate disaster risk assessments (Alexander et al., 2023; Gwon et al., 2022; Hoerold et al., 2021; Leary et al., 2023; Sarmiento et al., 2019; Shweta et al., 2022; T. Oyama et al., 2021). This hindered the development of a stable and resilient business environment.

Chapter 4 discussed the data findings and how they were organized into themes and sub-themes to address the research questions. The analysis was based on interviews with eight SME owners and managers, focusing on technology-driven disaster preparedness. The study's trustworthiness was ensured through credibility, confirmability, dependability, and transferability (Bloomberg, 2022), validating the value of qualitative research. Semi-structured interviews provided rich data, with two SME leaders contributing significantly to technology-driven preparedness.

The study was guided by the COR theory (Hobfoll, 1989), which helped narrow the focus and provided a structured approach. Transcripts were sent to participants for member checking, and the data were analyzed using NVivo software, identifying 42 codes across seven categories. These codes were distilled into two main themes:

Theme 1: Technology-Driven Disaster Preparedness Integration: SME owners, leaders, and stakeholders' understanding from lessons learned, the importance of mitigating disaster preparedness barriers and constraints by investing in business resilience and remediating disaster risk through BC and DR.

Theme 2: Fostering an Innovative Preparedness Culture: Fostering innovative disaster preparedness solutions as a culture adhering to integrating tailored training and prioritizing BC should be understood by the SME workforce.

Key findings included the importance of identifying effective and affordable disaster solutions, overcoming constraints, and integrating innovative preparedness strategies. The study also underscored the role of government support and the necessity of prioritizing BC. Chapter 4 presented the emergence of sub-themes and the comprehensive findings, setting the stage for the next chapter, which discusses practical implications, recommendations, and future research.

Implications, Recommendations, and Conclusions

In this chapter, we discuss the implications, presenting a comparison and contrast of the developed Research Questions (RQ) 1, RQ1a, RQ2, and RQ2a by categorizing findings into sub-themes and themes, recommendations for practice, recommendations for future research, and conclusion. The problem addressed in this study was Tennessee SME owners' challenges face while implementing innovative disaster preparedness solutions, which often result in early business closures, job losses, and negatively impacting the state's economy (Coates et al., 2019; J. Ha et al., 2022; Sarmiento et al., 2019; T. Oyama et al., 2021).

The purpose of this qualitative exploratory case study was to examine how the implementation of innovative disaster preparedness solutions by Tennessee SME owners through mitigatory strategies against the challenges faced enhanced business resilience and facilitated effective responses against disasters. The qualitative research methodology selected was the most appropriate for the study, and the exploratory case study design indicated how the research problem would be addressed to determine the need for more technology-driven disaster preparedness solutions implemented by Tennessee SME owners. The qualitative exploratory case study provided in-depth research that reported findings using narrative methods (Bloomberg, 2022).

For the exploratory case study, the qualitative researcher presented a detailed analysis of sub-themes and themes from the data collected, including the lessons learned from a bounded case and its context (Bloomberg, 2022; Yin, 2018). This included several samples while creating storytelling summaries. The selected exploratory case study design presented in-depth research since the design is defined with a boundary setting to clarify the study phenomenon.

Data were collected using semi-structured interviews with a population sample of eight voluntary participants represented as SME owners and managers. Small business owners and managers were recruited using the created recruitment emails to participate in the research study. Informed consent was shared with recruited participants before the semi-structured interviews began using Zoom video or audio calls.

Some participants requested the interview questions in advance prior to participating in the semi-structured interviews. The semi-structured interview sessions lasted 45-60 minutes. The collected data were transcribed using Otter.ai and, upon completion, were forwarded to each participant for member checking. Subsequently, upon receiving the reviewed member checking transcripts from participants, they were uploaded to the NVivo software, whereby the data coding and analysis process began, and codes were categorized according to identified similarities to develop subthemes and themes.

The final section of Chapter 5 was the conclusion, which was presented in detail, with the study implications indicating factors that could have influenced the interpretation of the results. Additionally, in Chapter 5, the qualitative researcher elaborated on the following areas: an introduction and reiteration of the problem addressed, a purpose statement, the implications of the study, recommendations for practice and future research, a conclusion, and the importance of the study.

Subsequently, the overall message learned from the study was added to the conclusion of Chapter 5, with detailed emphasis on the study results and their implications. These findings were consistent with existing literature and theories related to theoretical preparedness.

Implications

This exploratory case study, guided by the COR theory, highlighted how SME owners should integrate innovative disaster preparedness solutions for business-responsive readiness to enhance business resilience while preserving valuable assets (Hobfoll et al., 2018; Serenko et al., 2024; T. Oyama et al., 2021). This approach emphasized the importance of adopting advanced technologies and frameworks to mitigate the impacts of disasters and ensure business continuity.

By aligning with COR theoretical principles, the study provided a robust framework for understanding how SMEs can effectively manage and protect their resources in the face of disaster (C. Wang et al., 2023; Cai et al., 2023; Nath et al., 2024; T. Oyama et al., 2021). The COR theory provided a strong foundation for the process where SME owners should begin implementing innovative and technology-driven disaster preparedness solutions, determined to preserve valuable assets (Nath et al., 2024).

The implications of this study extend beyond individual SME owners to the broader economic and social landscape. The research underscored SME owners' need to invest in technology-driven disaster preparedness solutions to safeguard their operations and contribute to the broader community's resilience. Thereby aligning with the literature findings that stressed the importance of integrating innovative disaster preparedness strategies within the broader context of government policies and frameworks (Cai et al., 2023; Nath et al., 2024; Serenko et al., 2024; T. Oyama et al., 2021).

Moreover, the study revealed significant barriers and constraints SME owners face in implementing innovative disaster preparedness solutions. The challenges, including time constraints, limited resources, and disasters emotional and psychological impact of disasters, highlight the need for tailored support and interventions. This finding has broader implications for policymakers and support organizations, suggesting that more comprehensive and accessible resources are needed to support SME owners in overcoming these obstacles and improving disaster preparedness (T. Oyama et al., 2021).

Additionally, the broader social and ethical ramifications of the study's recommendations are profound. By fostering readiness training and creating safe spaces for employees, businesses can significantly enhance community resilience and protect the workforce's well-being. This ethical consideration aligned with the trauma-informed positive education (TIPE) model, promoting the protection and education of vulnerable employees (Alexander & Harris, 2020).

The use of advanced technologies such as artificial intelligence (AI) and blockchain for consistent monitoring and data aggregation further underscores the critical role of innovation in disaster preparedness (Ali et al., 2021; Shweta et al., 2022). Conversely, the use of advanced technologies as a responsive solution, which is often used by the incident response team in times of uncertainty, demonstrated how vigilant the workforce is prepared for disastrous situations.

The study's qualitative research methodological rigor contributed to its reliability and trustworthiness. It ensured credibility through member checking, transferability with a clear audit trail, dependability via detailed audit processes, and confirmability through transparent journaling and coding practices. The research maintained high standards of qualitative inquiry (Bloomberg, 2022). The research methodology approach strengthened the study's findings and provided a model for future research in the field.

Therefore, this study's broader significance lies in its potential to inform policy changes, enhance support systems for SMEs, and foster community resilience through innovative disaster preparedness solutions. By addressing barriers and leveraging the insights from the COR theory, future research can build on this foundation to develop more effective and sustainable disaster preparedness and response strategies.

This study advanced the COR theory by demonstrating its application in disaster preparedness among SMEs, highlighting the practical implications of resource preservation during disruptive events. The study's findings indicated challenges in recruiting SME owners due to time constraints and business closures after experiencing a disastrous event, which hindered progress. Despite these obstacles, the study's trustworthiness remained intact through rigorous methodologies like member checking, audit trails, and transparent journaling (Bloomberg, 2022).

The researcher managed personal biases by reflecting on potential sampling influences and maintaining thorough data collection, coding, and analysis processes. The broader significance of this study lies in its implications for policy changes, support systems for SMEs, and community resilience. By critically analyzing these findings, the research underscored the importance of innovative, technology-driven disaster preparedness solutions and tailored interventions to manage resources effectively during disruptions (Cai et al., 2023; Hobfoll et al., 2018; Nath et al., 2024).

This approach strengthens the study's contributions to the existing literature and provides actionable insights for future research and policy development. This section entailed the implications of the study. Thirty-one codes were grouped around the research questions into sub-themes and themes.

The sub-themes emerged from the research into seven sub-themes:

(a) Lessons learned from disastrous events;

(b) Barriers and constraints hindering the implementation of technology-driven disaster preparedness solutions;

(c) Integration of innovative technology-driven solutions promoting business resilience;

(d) Disastrous events impacting business continuity (BC);

(e) Implementing innovatively tailored preparedness training;

(f) BC prioritization following a disastrous event; and

(g) Preparedness procedures promoting the integration of disaster preparedness training.

The exploratory case study offered valuable and strategic insights into the challenges hindering Tennessee SME owners from implementing innovative and technology-driven disaster preparedness solutions. The implications were derived from the findings, consistent with the literature data findings in the study.

Two themes emerged after categorizing the analyzed data: (a) Theme 1, From lessons learned, SME owners and managers understood the importance of implementing technology-driven disaster preparedness solutions against barriers and constraints through mitigatory strategies, such as investing in business resilience, remediating disaster risk, and integrating BC and DR; and (b) Theme 2, Fostering innovative disaster preparedness solutions as a culture adhering to integrating tailored training and prioritizing BC should be understood by the SME workforce.

RQ1.

How do Tennessee SME Owners Implement Innovative And Technology-Driven Disaster Preparedness Solutions to Address Challenges Faced During The Preservation of Valuable Resources?

RQ1a.

How do Tennessee SME Owners Integrate Effective Processes to Remediate Challenging Barriers or Resource Constraints that Continue Hindering The Implementation of Technology-Driven Disaster Preparedness Solutions? **Theme 1** emerged from data collected responding to RQ1 and RQ1a presented: From lessons learned, SME owners and managers understood the importance of implementing technology-driven disaster preparedness solutions against barriers and constraints through mitigatory strategies, such as investing in business resilience, remediating disaster risk, and integrating BC and DR. In Theme 1, the findings indicated that Tennessee SME owners should implement technology-driven disaster preparedness solutions to protect and preserve valuable assets and their workforce against disastrous events despite their challenges.

Theme 1: **SME Owners' Understanding From Lessons Learned to Ensure Technology-Driven Disaster Preparedness Solutions Were Implemented Against Barriers And Constraints Using Mitigatory Strategies.** The research findings highlighted SME owners' barriers and challenges, revealing valuable lessons learned from past disasters. These insights shaped the integration of mitigation strategies and informed investments in efficient procedures to implement technology-driven solutions for disaster preparedness.

According to the data collection findings, SME owners and managers demonstrated an understanding of integrating innovative disaster preparedness solutions. However, they continue to face numerous business constraints that pose significant challenges. The study's most significant implications and consequences, both positive and negative to SME owners or desired organizational outcomes, are distinguished between probable and improbable implications. This could have practical implications on BC, workforce safety, and revenue growth for SMEs. In addition, there may also be an implication for further research into why the lack of technology-driven disaster preparedness integration appears to persist in higher numbers for small businesses in Tennessee.

Understanding Barriers Hindering the Integration of Preparedness Solutions

The study highlighted a significant barrier hindering SME owners and managers from adopting technology-driven disaster preparedness solutions, such as financial constraints. The consistent finding that many SME owners lack the financial resources to invest in innovative technologies suggests a critical need for financial support mechanisms. These identified financial support programs include government grants, low-interest loans, or incentives for SMEs to adopt advanced disaster preparedness frameworks.

This was consistent in the Chapter 2 literature review discussed by Mishra et al. (2023), which presented barriers that could be mitigated through government regulations, legal barriers, and support to address limitations introduced by disastrous impacts. Small business owners face challenges that can be mitigated with constrained resources, which is consistent with the literature (Asgary et al., 2020; Eggers, 2020; J. Ha et al., 2022; Mishra et al., 2023; Q. S. A. Ali et al., 2023).

The barriers SME owners face are uncontrollable and are, in most cases, unaffordable for small business budgets. Mishra et al. (2023) reiterated the importance of mitigating risks and resolving the barriers challenging SME owners. The challenges of disaster risks deter SMEs' revenue growth and must be mitigated to compete with evolving markets, which should be approached strategically (Gwon et al., 2022; Lee & Chen, 2021; T. Oyama et al., 2021; Tosun & Bostan, 2021).

Importance of Business Resilience

Technologically innovative tools have been shown to mitigate risks and vulnerabilities, as identified by SME owners and incident response teams, leading to accurate and effective disaster preparedness solutions (Ali et al., 2021; Bourdin et al., 2024; Shweta et al., 2022). These studies emphasized the importance of implementing technology-driven and resilient maturity models to sustain organizations from disaster risks impacting SME business growth. For instance, during times of uncertainty, incident response teams confirmed that AI and blockchain forecasting tools were effective due to their reliability in monitoring readiness and accurately aggregating data (Ali et al., 2021; Bourdin et al., 2024; Shweta et al., 2022).

It is essential to thoroughly assess data collected through continuous monitoring, especially when inaccuracies arise, to avoid implementing ineffective mitigation strategies. Such missteps could impede SME owners' efforts to integrate technology-driven disaster preparedness solutions and safeguard their resource investments.

This study emphasized adopting these solutions to shield the workforce from disruptive events. Additionally, it advocated for implementing a trauma-informed positive education (TIPE) model to introduce knowledge-based interventions and support vulnerable employees (Alexander & Harris, 2020). The proactive establishment of readiness frameworks and policies by SME owners was found to motivate employees both before and after a disaster, significantly contributing to recovery efforts in the aftermath of disruptive events.

Integrating Emerging Technologies

Small business owners acknowledged the value of strengthening business resilience by adopting a proactive mindset toward disaster preparedness solutions. This finding suggests that educational programs emphasizing risk management, business continuity (BC) planning, and disaster recovery (DR) can effectively support the adoption of technology-driven solutions. Furthermore, SME owners and stakeholders gain valuable insights through collaborations with academic institutions or consulting firms specializing in these fields.

Asgary et al. (2020) emphasized the importance of fostering advanced disaster preparedness frameworks and policy solutions as readiness strategies and outlining the implementation of readiness tools such as robotics, drones, automation, and artificial intelligence to maximize organizational resilience. Small businesses' integration of emerging technologies merged with innovative disaster preparedness solutions will promote organizational resilience and increase revenue growth (Asgary et al., 2020; F. Ali et al., 2023). Small business resilience was discussed to be strengthened using backup procedures, cloud computing, and trending technologies such as artificial intelligence (AI) driven tools, robotics, and drones, as identified by a few participants from the data findings.

Small business owners and managers' initiatives to implement technology-driven disaster preparedness and innovative solutions mitigated disaster risks and vulnerabilities using disaster risk monitoring tools (Asgary et al., 2020; Q. S. A. Ali et al., 2023). If a resilient disaster preparedness strategy is integrated within an organization, revenue growth will be generated due to stability and BC, further boosting the state's economy.

Utilization of Rainy Day Fund (RDF) and Other Policies and Frameworks

The RDF framework was implied as an important solution for SME owners during or after experiencing a disruptive event for BC and other purposes to avoid business closure or during DR, as the organizations continue operations, as confirmed by Participant P5. The research finding was consistent with the literature whereby innovative disaster preparedness strategies such as RDF and Disaster Preparedness Guide (DPG) developed by FEMA were integrated to mitigate disaster risks by remediating financial limitations following a disastrous event (J. Ha et al., 2022; Lee & Chen, 2021; Sarmiento et al., 2019).

SME owners' investment in RDF frameworks and policies offered a robust strategy to continue business operations and mitigate disastrous impacts, as confirmed by participants in terms of the financial aspect. This indicates a broader implication for SME owners in establishing and promoting RDF frameworks and policies as part of the overall disaster risk management strategy. Additionally, further research may be warranted into the effectiveness of RDFs in different sectors and best practices for implementation. Moreover, the study findings were consistent with the literature identifying RDF as an essential tool for SME owners as a preparedness solution to mitigate business structure against total loss while avoiding early business closure (Lee & Chen, 2021).

Collaborative Networks

During data collection, participants explained determining disaster preparedness strategies with key stakeholders, implying the importance of collaboration among SME owners, managers, and stakeholders. Conversely, the developed networks and partnerships will facilitate shared learning and resource pooling. Therefore, adapting collaborative network efficiency for technology-driven disaster preparedness solutions bolsters SME workforce readiness posture against disruptive events, including a smooth BC transition sustaining organizational operations (Gwon et al., 2022; Leary et al., 2023; Saad et al., 2021; T. Oyama et al., 2021; Tosun & Bostan, 2021).

SME owners could benefit from community-based workshops or forums to discuss best practices and innovative solutions for disaster preparedness. Sarmiento et al. (2019) indicated how SME owners invest minimal efforts in collaborative efforts, whereas networking capabilities can improve business readiness to face future challenges. Communicating reliably enabled SME owners and suppliers to be safe while adhering to best practices and a collaborative approach, specifically with secure and confidential outcomes (Ali et al., 2021; Green, 2023; Hsu & Sharma, 2023; Shweta et al., 2022).

Government and Nonprofit Support

According to the research findings, government agencies provided supportive incentivized programs, policies, and frameworks for SMEs to boost business resilience. Additionally, SME owners offered financial support following disastrous events, especially for high-risk SME owners who often face crises (Eggers, 2020). The reliance on government programs, such as the PPP loans, highlighted the importance of external financial support systems; therefore, one of the most important implications this study focused on was ensuring SME owners are aware of government agencies such as FEMA that provide preparedness assistance for disaster readiness including policy templates, frameworks, and training programs.

Other policies and frameworks provided by government agencies to businesses include the RDF and DPG (J. Ha et al., 2022; Lee & Chen, 2021; Sarmiento et al., 2019). SME owners' integration of preparedness solutions with the NDRF, also established by FEMA, provided guidance for mitigatory strategies against vulnerabilities and expedited recovery efforts following a disastrous event (J. Ha et al., 2022; Lee & Chen, 2021). This was consistent with research findings.

Humanistic Approach to Data Collection

The use of a humanistic approach in the qualitative research study and data collection procedure reinforced the need to capture the lived experiences of SME owners during crises (Bloomberg, 2022). The perspective leads to more nuanced insights crucial for developing effective support programs. Future studies should continue to prioritize the voices of SME owners to inform accurate integration of the effectiveness of innovative disaster preparedness policies and practices.

Bloomberg (2022) highlighted the significance of the human element in research, emphasizing its crucial role in shaping the interpretation of collected data. Consequently, maintaining an open mind and applying critical thinking when assessing findings, especially when considering alternative perspectives, is essential (Bloomberg, 2022). To ensure a comprehensive analysis, the researcher had to avoid relying on a simplistic linear approach.

RQ2.

In What Ways Do Tennessee SME Owners And Incident Response Workforce Embrace an Innovative Technology-Driven Disaster Preparedness Solutions-Oriented Culture Within Their Organizations?

RQ2a.

How do Tennessee SME Owners Integrate COR Theoretical Principles And Corollaries Within Organizations to Preserve Valuable Resources By Implementing Innovative Disaster Preparedness Solutions?

One theme emerged from RQ2: Theme 2 indicated SME workforce understands the solution of fostering an innovative disaster preparedness culture by adhering to integrated, tailored training and prioritizing BC. In Theme 2, the findings indicated fostering innovative disaster preparedness solutions as a culture adhering to integrating tailored training and prioritizing BC should be understood by the SME workforce. The workforce disaster preparedness training pointed to focused technology-driven readiness, aiming at protecting employee safety as paramount, followed by preserving and protecting valuable resources, critical assets, and data.

Theme 2: Fostering Innovative Disaster Preparedness Solutions As a Culture Adhering to Integrating Tailored Training and Prioritizing BC Should Be Understood by The SME workforce. The study's implications regarding integrating technology-driven disaster preparedness training within the incident response workforce provided critical insight for SME owners looking to enhance their resilience against disruptive events through preparedness training programs. The data collection results implied from the findings the importance of SME owners and the workforce understanding the criticality of protecting employees through effective preparedness training for readiness against disastrous events. Implications were drawn from Theme Two findings in response to RQ2 and RQ2a.

Technology-Driven Preparedness Training and Awareness

Although low confidence was evident among most participants on the integration of technology-driven disaster preparedness solutions and training, data analysis for the information collected indicated that participants required readiness education and awareness programs. To mitigate the challenges faced by SME owners, according to the data collected from participants, adequate preparation for disruption indicated the importance of creating an organization that was capable of attracting and empowering the workforce with resilience and eagerness to learn with a sense of service (Leary et al., 2023).

Small business owners' establishment of a committed incident response team, mainly focused on innovative disaster preparedness integration and strengthening business resilience, was paramount for revenue growth and stabilized business operations (Alexander et al., 2023; Leary et al., 2023; Shweta et al., 2022; T. Oyama et al., 2021). Resilient programs, including frameworks and policies, were promoted by SME owners to mitigate disaster risks and recovery (Alexander et al., 2023; Gwon et al., 2022; Hoerold et al., 2021; Leary et al., 2023; Sarmiento et al., 2019; Shweta et al., 2022; T. Oyama et al., 2021). Open-sourced and government-provided preparedness training on the latest technology solutions for disaster preparedness was evident in empowering SME owners as they made informed decisions. Workshops and training sessions highlighted successful case studies to encourage greater adoption.

Emphasis on Tailored Training Programs

An established incident response workforce evaluated imminent disastrous events within the organization's geographical surroundings, whereby, following a disruptive event, post-recovery planning and training were adopted (Alexander et al., 2023; Green, 2023). The study emphasized workforce adept in disaster preparedness is critical for maintaining BC. According to the research findings, SME owners discussed the importance of developing and integrating effective, tailored training programs focused on their operations' specific needs and risks. Such training included simulations, workshops, and real-life scenario planning, engaged employees, and reinforced their skills in disaster crisis response.

Like the study findings, Leary et al. (2023) iterated that SME owners would invest in disaster preparedness training professionals to efficiently provide awareness to the organizational workforce, strengthening employees' resilience efforts. The contrast between participants who reported the existence of effective preparedness training was a ratio of 3:5, with the highest number indicating a significant training gap. This disparity underscores the need for SME owners to assess their current training initiatives and invest in comprehensive disaster preparedness training. Conversely, identifying best practices from those with effective training can help improve programs across the board.

Cultivating an Innovative Disaster Preparedness Culture

The findings highlighted the necessity of fostering an innovative culture around disaster preparedness within SMEs. This implies business owners should focus on compliance and encourage workforce readiness, engagement, creativity, and adaptability. Leadership should promote an environment where employees feel empowered to propose new ideas and innovative solutions for disaster preparedness, thus enhancing the organization's overall resilience. Eggers (2020) iterated that innovatively motivated SME owners should consider implementing disaster preparedness training solutions among employees despite disruptive crises.

Impact of Communication on BC Planning

Data collected indicated the detrimental effects of ineffective or ineffective communicative tools during disastrous events. This highlighted the need for SME owners to establish robust communication protocols, ensuring information flows seamlessly during crises (Green, 2023). Training included strategies for maintaining effective communication among teams and stakeholders to facilitate quick decision-making and coordinated responses. Green (2023) emphasized the importance of sharing data between suppliers and organizations, enhancing collaborative efforts, and reducing costs. However, data loss risks and misuse affected business-critical data integrity and confidentiality. Integrating BCM and DRR frameworks promoted business resilience against disaster risk while effectively enabling DR procedures (Sarmiento et al., 2019).

Investment in Technology-Driven Solutions

The literature presented a need to invest in technology-driven readiness solutions by SME owners, which can lead to ineffective disaster risk assessments; therefore, SME owners should strive to integrate mitigatory strategies (Shweta et al.,

2022). The study's findings implied SME owners must prioritize financial and strategic investments in technology-driven disaster preparedness solutions to enhance readiness capabilities. This could involve adopting new risk assessment software, incident response communication tools, and technologies to streamline recovery processes.

Strengthening Incident Response Workforce

Developing a resilient workforce environment empowered SMEs to transition and sustain business operations following a disastrous event (Gwon et al., 2022; Leary et al., 2023; Saad et al., 2021; T. Oyama et al., 2021; Tosun & Bostan, 2021). The findings reinforced the importance of a well-trained incident response workforce, as highlighted by the participants who confirmed practical disaster preparedness training. This implies that SME owners should consider designating specific roles or teams responsible for disaster preparedness and response.

By strengthening these teams through continuous and consistent readiness awareness education and training, SME incident response teams can effectively enhance their ability to respond to disastrous events (Tosun & Bostan, 2021). The incident response workforce followed a well-developed preparedness plan beginning with identifying disaster risks and vulnerabilities the organization was exposed to, with remediation solutions (Ali et al., 2021; Gwon et al., 2022; Shweta et al., 2022; T. Oyama et al., 2021; Tosun & Bostan, 2021).

Partnerships for Training and Development

To overcome limitations in resources and expertise, an additional implication of SME owners should seek partnerships with external organizations, such as local universities, industry associations, or government agencies, to facilitate training and training initiatives. Alexander and Harris (2020) agreed on the criticality of integrating crisis management to promote professional development for crisis management, to offer a wide range of resourceful training programs within organizations by SME owners. Collaborative efforts provided SME owners access to resources, expert knowledge, and a support network, enhancing the preparedness culture, which was consistent with the data collected and the literature findings.

Continuous Assessment and Improvement

The lack of effective training programs implied SME owners understood the importance of integrating continuous evaluations and improvements in disaster preparedness programs. SME owners' integration of continuous training procedures for regularly evaluating a readiness posture and strategies was considered essential for small businesses (Alexander & Harris, 2020). Training programs should be incorporated following feedback outcomes from the workforce during the adaptation of evolving procedures for readiness education in response to disaster risks and organizational preparedness needs.

Overall, the implications drawn from this exploratory case study highlighted a multifaceted approach for SME owners to implement innovative and technology-driven disaster preparedness solutions to mitigate disaster risk. The qualitative researcher explored the implications for RQ1 and RQ1a, identified mitigatory strategies against financial barriers, and promoted resilience and leadership decisions as essential steps toward SME owners' implementation of preparedness solutions against future disruptive events. Conversely, the implications from RQ2 and RQ2a suggested

SME owners need to adopt effective training programs and provide educational resources to foster innovative disaster preparedness solutions proactively. SME owners should build a resilient workforce capable of navigating disruptive events by prioritizing tailored training, fostering an influential readiness culture, enhancing communication capabilities as an investment in technology-driven preparedness solutions, and preserving valuable assets guided by the COR theory (Hobfoll, 2001). Such initiatives are essential for ensuring BC planning and minimizing disastrous impacts on organizational stability.

Recommendations for Practice

Based on the findings from the exploratory case study on the importance of implementing technology-driven disaster preparedness solutions by Tennessee SME owners, six recommendations for practice were developed. The recommendations referenced the study's research questions, findings, and themes. Conversely, the practice recommendations were categorized into topics, some of which developed from findings that were consistent with the literature; these comprised of the following areas:

(a) Enhancing financial support mechanisms,

(b) Fostering collaborative networks and strengthening communication protocols,

(c) Promoting business resilience through training development;

(d) Leveraging government and nonprofit resources;

(e) Investing in technology-driven solutions; and

(f) Continuously assessing and improving disaster preparedness strategies.

Step-by-step disaster preparedness solutions tailored explicitly towards unique barriers and constraints for Tennessee SME owners should be adopted to strengthen organizational operations, market share, and development of new products, guided by the COR theoretical principles and corollaries protecting valuable resources (Hobfoll, 2001). The free disaster preparedness tool provided by Ready (2023), "A Ready Business," outlines five critical steps that SME owners in Tennessee should introduce to mitigate disaster risk (Ready, 2023).

These steps include:

(a) Establishing management programs to organize, create, and foster disaster preparedness.

(b) Conducting a business impact analysis to assess disaster risk, identify potential disasters, and determine ways to mitigate these risks.

(c) Integrating a comprehensive preparedness plan that includes crisis communication, emergency response, business continuity, employee safety, resource preservation, information technology, incident response, and training documentation.

(d) Performing tabletop exercises to execute the documented preparedness plans and evaluate necessary changes to the preparedness management plan.

(e) Reviewing and developing improvement solutions to evaluate the program, using the results to make necessary changes and improvements.

By implementing these steps, SME owners can better prepare for and respond to disasters, ultimately safeguarding their business operations and resources (Ready, 2023). Therefore, a step-by-step process needs to be established in small businesses to prepare for and continue business operations following a disastrous event. It works in tandem with future recommendations.

Immediate Actions

Foster Collaborative Networks and Strengthen Communication Protocols

Organizations must foster a collaborative network among SME owners to develop early outreach and support small business owners and managers. The recommendation for practice-related data findings is to facilitate networking opportunities by developing communication planning platforms for SME owners to collaborate, share resources, and discuss disaster preparedness as best practices. This recommendation presented how benefits can be achieved through industry associations and community organizations (Green, 2023).

Conversely, collaborative efforts with academic institutions and consulting firms enabled relevant, expert-led training for SME owners, with other organizations to identify efficient disaster preparedness solutions. According to Green (2023), collaborative efforts should be sustained due to their importance among SME owners and suppliers, emphasizing the need for organizations to adopt SRM practices by assessing threat vulnerabilities for effective communication with suppliers.

Clear communication is essential for timely information delivery (Green, 2023). Establishing and strengthening communication protocols was essential for institutions such as schools and healthcare organizations, whereby state and federal departments provide a wide range of technology-driven and innovatively evolving resources (Alexander & Harris, 2020). Developing robust communication plans was essential and was included in the implications and recommendations for practice to ensure SME owners implemented clear communication protocols for disastrous situations and the workforce understood their roles and responsibilities. Training on communication tools promoted preparedness and awareness for integrating practical communicative tools for disastrous situations and ensured information was shared effectively.

Promote Business Resilience Through Training

The data findings supported the following recommendations for practice focused on developing education programs by SME owners, creating training modules focused on managing disaster risks, BC planning, and DR (Mishrif & Khan, 2023). This recommendation was supported by encouraging peer learning through forums or roundtable discussions, such as tabletop exercises, where SME owners learned from collaborative leaders' experiences and strategies for innovative disaster preparedness solutions. Conversely, implementing workshops and seminars organized by community-based workshops enabled SME owners to share experiences and strategies related to business resilience with managers and the workforce for effective disaster preparedness.

Mishrif and Khan (2023) stressed that SME owners should integrate workshops, readiness training, and technology-driven disaster preparedness with implementing mandatory policies. Developing training and partnership development was a recommendation for practice, enabling collaboration with educational institution partners, local universities, museums, and technical schools to develop training programs that will provide practical, hands-on experience in disaster preparedness (Tosun & Bostan, 2021).

In addition, engaging industry associations to create training initiatives was shared across small businesses to enhance overall disaster preparedness among the SME sector. Implementing innovative disaster preparedness-tailored training programs met the specific needs of the SME workforce, focused on operational disaster risks and mitigatory requirements using a mix of simulations, workshops, and scenario planning to engage employees. SME owners should incorporate technology-driven preparedness training on the latest technology solutions for disaster preparedness, ensuring the workforce is equipped to use emerging readiness tools (Mishrif & Khan, 2023).

Medium-Term Actions

Continuous Assessment And Improvement

The final recommendation for practice that coincides with Theme 1 from Lessons Learned as mitigatory strategies, wherein SME owners' continuous assessment and improvement processes guide, review, and update disaster preparedness strategies based on new information and changing risks. The study promoted SME owners' implementation of innovative disaster preparedness solutions against disastrous events affecting the workforce, whereby a trauma-informed positive education (TIPE) model was recommended to introduce training knowledge for employees (Alexander & Harris, 2020). Therefore, collecting employee feedback created mechanisms for collecting assessments from the workforce regarding the effectiveness of disaster preparedness programs, which will promote experiences and insights to inform ongoing improvements.

These recommendations aimed to equip Tennessee SME owners with the tools, knowledge, and resources to improve their disaster preparedness efforts. By addressing financial constraints, promoting resilience, fostering collaboration, and emphasizing tailored training, SME owners enhance organizational capacity to navigate disruptive events successfully. Implementing these strategies is essential for BC, minimizing adverse effects and enabling organizational stability and resilience. Kallmuenzer et al. (2024) elaborated on the importance of digitization, requiring technology professionals, SME owners, and managers to struggle to fulfill this need due to the lack of financial resources; therefore, investing in disaster risk preparedness assessment is not an option.

Leverage Government And Nonprofit Resources

Maximizing awareness of government-offered programs positions SME owners to be more informed about government-offered disaster preparedness incentives, policies, frameworks, training programs, and financial assistance resources available for all businesses (J. Ha et al., 2022; Lee & Chen, 2021; Sarmiento et al., 2019). This coincided with the data findings collected from participants. Partnering with nonprofits through collaborative efforts provides SME owners access by exchanging information as soon as government agencies, such as FEMA, release training resources and supportive services.

Disaster preparedness-oriented government agencies like FEMA provide financial programs and technical assistance, which are practical for SME owners in promoting investment in effective training and understanding the preservation of valuable resources (Mishrif & Khan, 2023; Tosun & Bostan, 2021). With government assistance, most SMEs should avoid negative, disastrous consequences with impacts affecting long-term business operations.

Long-Term Actions

Enhance Financial Support Mechanisms

Financial support capabilities should be established through financial assistance programs or integration of the RDF developed by FEMA, a government entity, to support SME owners as they adopt technology-driven disaster preparedness solutions (J. Ha et al., 2022; Lee & Chen, 2021; Sarmiento et al., 2019). Financial support ranges from grants to low-interest loans and tax incentives. In addition, SME owners should be educated on available resources through outreach campaigns that will inform business owners about existing financial support options, such as government grants, frameworks, nonprofit funding, and industry-specific financial assistance programs.

The recommendation for practice referenced for Theme 1, whereby findings were consistent with the literature discussed by Sarmiento et al. (2019) and Lee and Chen (2021). Financial lack continues to impact SME owners' implementation of mitigatory strategies such as policies, frameworks, and low-interest loans offered by government agencies and societal organizations possessing the capacity to support SMEs. For instance, the RDF framework is intended for emergency crises among SME budgets for disaster or emergency circumstances offered by state government agencies (Lee & Chen, 2021).

Advocating for RDF frameworks' integration by SME owners as part of disaster risk management strategies guided the effective creation and management of funds. The recommendation for practice is vital for integrating best practices by conducting studies identified as the most effective RDF models and frameworks in diverse sectors and providing SME owners with tailored strategies that can be quickly adopted. Likewise, frameworks and policies in tandem with the

RDF framework, including BC planning, were consistent with both data findings and the literature review, which were recognized to prepare SME owners and the workforce effectively for disastrous events (Ali et al., 2021; Shweta et al., 2022).

Invest In Technology-Driven Solutions

Another recommendation for practice involves prioritizing technology-driven investments by SME owners and allocating budget and resources to invest in readiness solutions enhancing organizational resilience, such as risk assessment software, incident response tools, and communication technologies. The recommendation for practice encouraged adopting best practices by sharing case studies and success stories of other SME owners, effectively guiding technology-driven preparedness solutions into effective strategies (Mishrif & Khan, 2023).

Technology-driven disaster preparedness contributions will improve SME owners, stakeholders, and incident response teams' understanding, as the study contributions indicate enhancing organizational operations and performance, maximizing the competitive marketplace. The study presented SME owners' possession of the advantage of investing and adopting innovatively emerging technology to accommodate disastrous crisis outcomes.

Recommendations for Future Research

Based on the theoretical framework, data collected, study findings, participant demographics, and implications of the exploratory case study, numerous opportunities for future related research were presented, and the importance of Tennessee SME owners' implementation of emerging technology-driven disaster preparedness solutions was highlighted. A qualitative and quantitative research study could have added valuable information to the body of knowledge for SME owners, scholars, organizations, incident response teams, emergency teams, consultants, and other professionals from different industries. In this section, the researcher provided a basis for future research recommendations.

Adopting Disaster Preparedness Training

Recommendations for future research underscore the importance of SME owners' and managers' implementation of technology-driven disaster preparedness solutions, including training programs to establish effective and robust incident response teams to strengthen organizational resilience further and increase revenue growth. The study findings indicated a gap in integrating disaster preparedness training programs, which can be mitigated by adopting innovative readiness programs focused on emerging technology-driven solutions.

For example, AI-powered simulation exercises, blockchain-based tracking systems for resource allocation, and mobile apps for real-time disaster response coordination could provide practical and scalable solutions for SME owners to enhance their implementation of disaster preparedness strategies (Shweta et al., 2022). In addition, effective monitoring and evaluation training procedures should be assessed using employee feedback to refine and improve readiness training processes.

Preservation of Valuable Resources

An additional recommendation for future research encouraged Tennessee SME owners to implement innovative technology-driven disaster preparedness solutions to preserve valuable resources in the organization, including workforce safety and preservation of critical data. Implementing disaster preparedness frameworks, such as BCM, is important because they promote business-critical operations continuity during or following disastrous events (Q. S. A. Ali et al., 2023). Effective BCM procedures, policies, and strategies integrated by SME owners promote business robustness while ensuring the continuity of essential operations persists when organizational resilience is established.

For instance, some SME owners disregarded the integration of BCM frameworks and practices mainly due to the lack of financial resources, revealing the preparedness gap in abilities to preserve valuable assets (Q. S. A. Ali et al., 2023; Ruiz-Cantisani et al., 2020; Tosun & Bostan, 2021). Financial limitations are a significant factor that continues to challenge

SME owners, setting barriers to investing in innovative disaster preparedness solutions. Similarly, current literature presented the scarcity of BCM frameworks within small businesses, pointing to the need to invest in effective BCM planning to promote disaster preparedness solutions, whereby future research must be continued.

Recruiting and Developing A Resilient Response Team

Developing a resilient incident response team is crucial for effective disaster preparedness and recovery. The team's primary function is to ensure that the SME workforce responds swiftly and effectively to disastrous events, minimizing the impact on business operations and ensuring the safety of employees and resources is preserved. The last recommendation for future research should present SME owners' understanding of the importance of investing in a disaster preparedness professional incident response team culture, including disaster risk mitigation and contingency planning (Alexander et al., 2023; Leary et al., 2023; Tosun & Bostan, 2021).

For example, targeted training initiatives and monitoring and evaluation procedures using digital technology should be integrated to assess the effectiveness of disaster preparedness programs and improve readiness training. These comprehensive approaches can guide SME owners to strengthen resilient organizations and ensure they are well-prepared for future disasters. Leary et al. (2023) agreed on the criticality of recruiting and developing a stable and committed disaster preparedness response team willing to learn and adjust to change during or after a disastrous event while keeping businesses resilient.

Incorporating disaster risk mitigation and contingency planning into disaster preparedness programs enabled the incident response team to adopt agile strategies, ensuring readiness for unforeseen disastrous circumstances that the workforce may not have been previously prepared to handle (Alexander et al., 2023; Leary et al., 2023; Tosun & Bostan, 2021). When SME owners do not invest in developing a preparedness incident response team, an increase in organizational challenges erupts, introducing challenges such as lack of BC initiatives, disaster recovery involvement, bankruptcies due to loss of valuable assets, and loss of employment, thereby leaned toward the relevance and converging of the COR theoretical framework determined for the study (Hobfoll, 1989).

Therefore, SME owners should promote robust training programs to build a resilient organizational incident response team and strengthen the workforce in a disaster preparedness mindset. Alexander et al. (2023) reaffirmed disaster preparedness education frameworks that lay out guided procedures for mitigating vulnerabilities, providing direction to disaster risk recovery, which can be helpful to SME owners.

Specific examples for enhancing the capabilities of an incident response team include (a) training and certification courses for team members, keeping them updated on the latest disaster response techniques and technologies such as the Incident Command System (ICS) or BCM to enhance team's expertise (Alexander et al., 2023); (b) simulation exercises preparing the team for various disaster scenarios.

These exercises can include tabletop drills, full-scale simulations, and virtual reality-based training to simulate real-life disaster conditions including AI-powered simulation tools are effective in realistic scenarios (Shweta et al., 2022); (c) technology integration to equip the incident response team with advanced technologies such as AI for predictive analytics blockchain, enhancing the team's ability to respond quickly and accurately during a disaster (Ali et al., 2021); (d) cross-training to ensure all members possess a broad understanding of different roles and responsibilities. This approach ensured that the team remained functional even if some members were unavailable during a disastrous event (Leary et al., 2023); (e) continuous improvement by regularly reviewing and updating the incident response plan based on feedback from team members and lessons learned from past incidents to refine training programs and strategies (Bloomberg, 2022); (f) collaboration with external agencies fostering strong relationships with local organizations, government agencies and other organizations involved in disaster response to enhance effectiveness during disasters (Alexander et al., 2023); and (g) psychological support recognizing the emotional and psychological impact of disasters on team members and provide access to mental health support and counseling services focused on building a resilient incident response team ensuring the well-being of its members (Leary et al., 2023).

By focusing on these areas, SME owners can build a strong and adaptable incident response team capable of handling various scenarios and promoting business continuity. These recommendations not only enhance the team's preparedness but also contribute to the overall resilience of the organization.

Conclusions

This study addressed the critical problem Tennessee SME owners faced when attempting to implement innovative disaster preparedness solutions, a challenge often resulting in early business closure, job losses, and negatively impacting the state's economy (Coates et al., 2019; J. Ha et al., 2022; Sarmiento et al., 2019; T. Oyama et al., 2021). By exploring the barriers and strategies for mitigating disaster risk, the purpose of this qualitative exploratory case study was to present how the implementation of technology-driven preparedness solutions can enhance business resilience and improve the ability of SME owners and leaders to respond effectively to disasters.

The findings highlight that while SME owners in Tennessee recognize the importance of disaster preparedness, they face significant obstacles, including financial constraints and a need for integrated technology-driven solutions. The barriers prevent many SME owners from implementing the necessary strategies to preserve their valuable resources and ensure BC in the face of disruptive events. Research question 1 (RQ1) explored how Tennessee SME owners could better implement innovative disaster preparedness solutions, and the data findings indicated the existence of awareness of the need for disaster preparedness; many SME owners pointed to the lack of financial resources and technological infrastructure to adopt these solutions.

The limitation often resulted in inadequate BC plans, leaving SMEs vulnerable to prolonged recovery or permanent closure following a disaster. Additionally, RQ1a examined how SME owners could successfully overcome barriers such as resource constraints to integrate technology-driven disaster preparedness solutions. The findings suggested that while some SMEs can leverage government support, partnerships, and internal savings, financial limitations still must be addressed. Only a few participants confirmed the availability of RDF frameworks or external financial support to mitigate disaster risk, which ultimately led to better preparedness and quicker recovery after events like the COVID-19 pandemic.

In response to RQ2, which explored how Tennessee SME owners and their incident response teams could adopt an innovative, technology-driven disaster preparedness culture, the study found that the organizational culture around preparedness needed to be more consistent. A few organizations demonstrated a strong disaster preparedness culture through tailored training and a focus on BC; others needed to be made aware of or underinvested in such training. This gap in preparedness was particularly evident in organizations that needed more disaster risk assessments or comprehensive preparedness strategies, ultimately hindering their ability to respond to and recover from disruptive events. RQ2a aimed to explore how SME owners could integrate the COR theory principles into their organizations, highlighting that preserving physical and financial resources is a central tenet of business resilience.

The study found that businesses that integrated COR principles, such as fostering resource conservation and investing in readiness measures, were better equipped to face disruptive events. However, many SME owners struggled to fully apply these principles due to the lack of available resources, underlining the need for more robust financial planning and external support. The research concluded with a critical insight: while Tennessee SME owners acknowledged the importance of disaster preparedness, there remains considerable opportunity for improvement in adopting innovative, technology-driven solutions, improving resource management, and enhancing workforce training programs.

The findings of this study revealed that integrating innovative disaster preparedness strategies, supported by financial investment and resilient organizational culture, enables SME owners and managers to develop effective mitigation frameworks using BC and DR policies to address and reduce the impact of disastrous events and their outcomes.

The findings of this study underscore the critical need for targeted policies and support systems to help SMEs navigate disaster preparedness. Policymakers can develop and implement frameworks that provide financial incentives, grants, and access to technology-driven preparedness solutions

(FEMA, 2023). Additionally, establishing partnerships between government agencies, NGOs, and the private sector can facilitate resource-sharing and collaborative efforts, enhancing SMEs' overall resilience in disaster-prone regions (Liang et al., 2023).

By promoting a culture of preparedness and ensuring access to necessary resources, SME owners can support small businesses to survive and thrive in the face of unforeseen challenges and strengthen the economic fabric of communities (Alisjahbana et al., 2022). Future research is still needed to explore how SME owners across different regions can implement these strategies more effectively, especially when facing financial challenges and limited access to technological resources. Ultimately, ensuring SME owners are better prepared will contribute to the long-term sustainability of small businesses and the broader state economy.

References

Adame, A. L., Perry, C., & Pierce, E. (2020). Community and housing first: A qualitative analysis of USA residents' perspectives. *Health & Social Care in the Community*, *28*(4), 1292–1300. https://doi.org/10.1111/hsc.12962

Akpinar, H., & Özer-Çaylan, D. (2023). Organizational resilience in maritime business: A systematic literature review. *Management Research Review*, *46*(2), 245–267. https://doi.org/10.1108/MRR-12-2021-0866

Alexander, B., Fordham, M., Jigyasu, R., Luneta, M., & Wisner, B. (2023). Twenty years of Radical Disaster Interpretations: Reflections and aspirations (RADIX @ 20!). Conversation on disasters: Deconstructed on 13 October 2021. *Disaster Prevention and Management*, *32*(3), 443–457. https://doi.org/10.1108/dpm-11-2022-0235

Alexander, B., & Harris, H. (2020). Public school preparedness for school shootings: A phenomenological overview of school staff perspectives. *School Mental Health*, *12*(3), 595–609. https://doi.org/10.1007/s12310-020-09369-8

Ali, F., Zhang, Z., & Akhtar, S. (2023). Exploring technology-driven disaster preparedness solutions. *Journal of Business Continuity and Emergency Planning, 15*(3), 123–135.

Ali, Q. S. A., Hanafiah, M. H., & Mogindol, S. H. (2023). Systematic literature review of business continuity management (BCM) practices: Integrating organizational resilience and performance in small and medium enterprises (SMEs) BCM framework. *International Journal of Disaster Risk Reduction, 99*, Article 104135. https://doi.org/10.1016/j.ijdrr.2023.104135

Ali, Z., Bi, G., & Mehreen, A. (2021). Do vulnerability mitigation strategies influence firm performance? The mediating role of supply chain risk. *International Journal of Emerging Markets, 18*(3), 748–767. https://doi.org/10.1108/ijoem-04-2020-0397

Alisjahbana, I., Moura-Cook, A., Costa, R., & Kiremidjian, A. (2022). An agent-based financing model for post-earthquake housing recovery: Quantifying recovery inequalities across income groups. *Earthquake*

Spectra, *38*(2), 1254–1282.
https://doi.org/10.1177/87552930211064319

Andrade, E. L., Cordova, A., Schagen, C. R. V., Jula, M., Rodriguez-Diaz, C. E., Rivera, M. I., & Santos-Burgoa, C. (2022). The impact of Hurricane Maria on individuals living with non-communicable disease in Puerto Rico: The experience of 10 communities. *BMC Public Health*, *22*(1), Article 2083. https://doi.org/10.1186/s12889-022-14552-4

Asgary, A., Özdemir, A., & Özyürek, H. (2020). Small and medium enterprises and global risks: Evidence from manufacturing SMEs in Turkey. *International Journal of Disaster Risk Science*, *11*(1), 59–73. https://doi.org/10.1007/s13753-020-00247-0

Barton-Hulsey, A., Boesch, M. C., Chung, Y., Caswell, T., Sonntag, A. M., & Quach, W. (2023). Emergency and disaster preparedness for individuals who use augmentative and alternative Communication: A pilot study on supported planning using a toolkit. *American Journal of Speech-Language Pathology*, *33*(1), 16–32. https://doi.org/10.1044/2023_ajslp-23-00086

Bazeley, P., & Jackson, K. (2013). *Qualitative data analysis with NVivo*. Sage.

Bengry-Howell, A., & Griffin, C. (2012). Negotiating access in ethnographic research with 'hard to reach' young people: establishing common ground or a process of methodological grooming? *International Journal of Social Research Methodology, 15*(5), 403–416.

Bloomberg, L. D. (2022). *Completing your qualitative dissertation: A road map from beginning to end,* 5–459.

Boutmaghzoute, H., & Moustaghfir, K. (2021). Exploring the relationship between corporate social responsibility actions and employee retention: A human resource management perspective. *Human Systems Management, 40*(6), 789–801. https://doi.org/10.3233/HSM-211202

Bourdin, M., Paviot, T., Pellerin, R., & Lamouri, S. (2024). NLP in SMEs for Industry 4.0: Opportunities and challenges. *Procedia Computer Science, 239*, 396–403. https://doi.org/10.1016/j.procs.2024.06.186

Cai, Z., Mao, Y., Gong, T., Xin, Y., & Lou, J. (2023). The effect of servant leadership on work resilience: Evidence from the hospitality industry during the COVID-19 period. *International Journal of Environmental Research and Public Health*, *20*(2), Article 1322. https://doi.org/10.3390/ijerph20021322

Caruth, G. D. (2015). Toward a conceptual model of ethics in research. *Journal of Management and Research*, *15*(1), 23–33. https://www.indianjournals.com/ijor.aspx?target=ijor:jmr&volume=15&issue=1&article=003

Chen, Y., Wang, C., Du, X., Shen, Y., & Hu, B. (2023). An agent-based simulation framework for developing the optimal rescue plan for older adults during the emergency evacuation. *Simulation Modelling Practice & Theory*, *128*, Article 102797. https://doi.org/10.1016/j.simpat.2023.102797

Coates, G., Li, C., Ahilan, S., Wright, N., & Alharbi, M. (2019). Agent-based modeling and simulation to assess flood preparedness and recovery of manufacturing small and medium-sized enterprises. *Engineering Applications of Artificial Intelligence*, *78*, 195–217. https://doi.org/10.1016/j.engappai.2018.11.010

Creswell, J. W. (2013). *Qualitative Inquiry and Research Design: Choosing Among Five Approaches*. Sage.

Creswell, J. W., & Creswell, J. D. (2017). *Research design: Qualitative, quantitative, and mixed methods approaches*. Sage publications.

Dalkin, S., Forster, N., Hodgson, P., Lhussier, M., & Carr, S. M. (2020). Using computer-assisted qualitative data analysis software (CAQDAS; NVivo) to assist in the complex process of realist theory generation, refinement, and testing. *International Journal of Social Research Methodology, 24*(1), 123–134. https://doi.org/10.1080/13645579.2020.1803528

Eckstein, S. (2003). The Belmont report: Ethical principles and guidelines for the protection of human subjects of research. In *Cambridge University Press eBooks* (pp. 126–132). https://doi.org/10.1017/cbo9780511550089.028

Eggers, F. (2020). Masters of disasters? Challenges and opportunities for SMEs in times of crisis. *Journal of Business Research, 116*, 199–208. https://doi.org/10.1016/j.jbusres.2020.05.025

Ešić, D., Nyberg, M., & Gallina, B. (2021). Product-line assurance cases from contract-based design. *Journal of Systems & Software, 176*, N.PAG. https://doi.org/10.1016/j.jss.2021.110922

FEMA (2023). *Grants for disaster preparedness and response*. Retrieved from https://www.fema.gov/

Gennari, F. (2022). The transition towards a circular economy. A framework for SMEs. *Journal of Management & Governance*, 1–35. https://doi.org/10.1007/s10997-022-09653-6

Gillani, M., Niaz, H. A., Farooq, M. U., & Ullah, A. (2022). Data collection protocols for VANETs: A survey. *Complex & Intelligent Systems, 8*(3), 2593–2622. https://doi.org/10.1007/s40747-021-00629-x

Giorgi, A. P., & Giorgi, B. (2008). Phenomenological psychology. *The SAGE handbook of qualitative research in psychology*, 165-178. https://doi.org/10.4135/9781848607927

Given, L. M. (2008). *The Sage encyclopedia of qualitative research methods*. Sage Publications.

Green, C. (2023). Best practices in supplier relationship management and response when supply is disrupted by cyber-attack: An incident response framework. *PubMed, 17*(1), 6–15. https://pubmed.ncbi.nlm.nih.gov/37537763

Guest, G., Bunce, A., & Johnson, L. (2006). How many interviews are enough? An experiment with data saturation and variability. *Field Methods, 18*(1), 59-82.

Gwon, S. H., Thongpriwan, V., Kett, P. M., & Cho, Y. (2022). Public health nurses' perceptions and experiences of emergency preparedness, responsiveness, and burnout during the COVID-19 pandemic. *Public Health Nursing, 40*(1), 124–134. https://doi.org/10.1111/phn.13141

Ha, J., Yun, J., & Lee, J. (2022). The impact of disaster preparedness on SME sustainability. *Small Business Economics, 50*(2), 321-333.

Ha, S., Childs, M., Kim, Y.-K., & Fairhurst, A. (2022). After the fire: An assessment of small business preparedness and recovery in Gatlinburg, Tennessee. *International Journal of Hospitality & Tourism Administration, 23*(2),

216–241.

https://doi.org/10.1080/15256480.2020.1727812

Heldring, S., Lindström, V., Jirwe, M., & Wihlborg, J. (2024).
Exploring ambulance clinicians' clinical reasoning when
training mass casualty incidents using virtual reality.
*Scandinavian Journal of Trauma Resuscitation and
Emergency Medicine, 32*(1).
https://doi.org/10.1186/s13049-024-01255-5

Hennink, M. M., Kaiser, B. N., & Marconi, V. C. (2016). Code
saturation versus meaning saturation. *Qualitative
Health Research, 27*(4), 591–608.
https://doi.org/10.1177/1049732316665344

Hiles, D., & Cermák, I. (2008). Narrative psychology. In *The
SAGE Handbook of qualitative research in psychology*
(pp. 147–64). SAGE Publications Ltd,
https://doi.org/10.4135/9781848607927

Hintz, E. A., & Dean, M. (2020). Best practices for returning
research findings to participants: Methodological and
ethical considerations for communication researchers.
Communication Methods & Measures, 14(1), 38–54.
https://doi.org/10.1080/19312458.2019.1650165

Hobfoll, S. E. (1989). Conservation of resources: A new

attempt at conceptualizing stress. *American*

Psychologist, 44(3), 513–524.

https://doi.org/10.1037/0003-066X.44.3.513

Hobfoll, S. E. (2001). The influence of culture, community, and

the nested self in the stress process: Advancing

conservation of resources theory. *Applied Psychology*,

50(3), 337–421. https://doi.org/10.1111/1464-

0597.00062

Hobfoll, S. E., Halbesleben, J., Neveu, J. P., & Westman, M.

(2018). Conservation of resources in the organizational

context: The reality of resources and their

consequences. *Annual Review of Organizational*

Psychology and Organizational Behavior, 5(1), 103-

128. https://doi.org/10.1146/annurev-orgpsych-032117-

104640

Hoerold, M., Gottschalk, M., Debbeler, C. M., Heytens, H.,

Ehrentreich, S., Braun-Dullaeus, R. C., & Apfelbacher,

C. (2021). Healthcare professionals' perceptions of

impacts of the COVID-19 pandemic on outpatient care

in rural areas: A qualitative study. *BMC Health Services*

Research, 21(1). https://doi.org/10.1186/s12913-021-07261-y

Hsu, J. L., & Sharma, P. (2023). Disaster and risk management in outdoor recreation and tourism in the context of climate change. *International Journal of Climate Change Strategies and Management, 15*(5), 712–728. https://doi.org/10.1108/ijccsm-10-2021-0118

Hummel-Rossi, B., McIlwain, C., & Mattis, J. (2006). *Quantitative research: Methods in the social sciences* [Video]. Sage Research Methods. https://doi.org/10.4135/9781483397160

Iphofen, R., & Tolich, M. (2018). *The Sage handbook of qualitative research ethics.* SAGE Publications Ltd. https://doi.org/10.4135/9781526435446

Jackson, D. P. (2024). *The impacts of change management processes on the organizational commitment of acquired management consultants during and after a merger and acquisition event* (Order No. 31298603). Available from Dissertations & Theses @ National University. (3074972860). https://go.openathens.net/redirector/nu.edu?url=https://

www.proquest.com/dissertations-theses/impacts-change-management-processes-on/docview/3074972860/se-2

Kallmuenzer, A., Mikhaylov, A., Chelaru, M., & Czakon, W. (2024). Adoption and performance outcome of digitalization in small and medium-sized enterprises. *Review of Managerial Science.* https://doi.org/10.1007/s11846-024-00744-2

Karlı, H., Savaş, S., & Tanyaş, M. (2022). Adoption of crowdsourced delivery: An online focus group interview. *Journal of Intelligent Transportation Systems & Applications*, 5(1), 70–85. https://doi.org/10.51513/jitsa.1079504

Karlı, L., Moin, S., & Cakmak, P. (2022). Enhancing disaster resilience through technology adoption in SMEs. *International Journal of Disaster Risk Reduction, 60*(1), 102-111.

Keidel, J., Bican, P. M., & Riar, F. J. (2021). Influential factors of network changes: Dynamic network ties and sustainable startup embeddedness. *Sustainability, 13*(11), 6184. https://doi.org/10.3390/su13116184

Kekeya, J. (2021). Qualitative case study research design: The commonalities and differences between collective, intrinsic, and instrumental case studies. *Contemporary PNG Studies*, *36*, 28–37.

Khurana, I., Dutta, D. K., & Singh Ghura, A. (2022). SMEs and digital transformation during a crisis: The emergence of resilience as a second-order dynamic capability in an entrepreneurial ecosystem. *Journal of Business Research*, *150*, 623–641. https://doi.org/10.1016/j.jbusres.2022.06.048

Leary, N., Perkins, L., Thakkar, U. G., & Gimpel, G. (2023). Build resilient enterprises with resilient people: The case of ASK Consulting. *Strategy & Leadership*, *51*(3), 27–30. https://doi.org/10.1108/sl-01-2023-0012

Lee, S., & Chen, G. (2021). Disaster experience and governments' savings: The moderating role of organizational capacity. *Journal of Public Administration Research and Theory*, *32*(3), 591–609. https://doi.org/10.1093/jopart/muab043

Liang, D., Ewing, B., Cardella, E., & Song, L. (2023). Probabilistic modeling of small business recovery after a hurricane: A case study of 2017 Hurricane Harvey. *Natural Hazards Review, 24*(1), 1–11. https://doi.org/10.1061/(ASCE)NH.1527-6996.0000602

Maluleka, S. M., & Ross, E. (2024). Ubuntu or Compliance? Knowledge, attitudes, and practices of owners of small and medium-sized enterprises in Johannesburg, South Africa regarding corporate social responsibility. *Journal of African Business*, 1–20. https://doi.org/10.1080/15228916.2024.2361504

Matthews-Trigg, N., Citrin, D., Halliday, S., Acharya, B., Maru, S., Bezruchka, S., & Maru, D. (2019). Understanding perceptions of global healthcare experiences on provider values and practices in the USA: A qualitative study among global health physicians and program directors. *BMJ Open, 9*(4), 1–8. https://doi.org/10.1136/bmjopen-2018-026020

McCourt, E. M., Singleton, J. A., Tippett, V., & Nissen, L. M. (2021). Exploring the factors affecting the preparedness of Australian pharmacists to respond to disasters: a qualitative study. *Journal of Pharmacy*

Practice and Research, *51*(2), 145–153.
https://doi.org/10.1002/jppr.1704

Mishra, M., Chaubey, A., Khatwani, R., & Nair, K. (2023).
Overcoming barriers in automotive SMEs to attain
international competitiveness: An ISM approach
modeling. *Journal of Business & Industrial Marketing*,
38(12), 2713–2730. https://doi.org/10.1108/jbim-12-
2022-0546

Mishrif, A., & Khan, A. (2023). Technology adoption as
survival strategy for small and medium enterprises
during COVID-19. *Journal of Innovation and
Entrepreneurship*, *12*(1).
https://doi.org/10.1186/s13731-023-00317-9

Mohajan, H. (2018). Qualitative research methodology in
social sciences and related subjects. *Journal of
Economic Development, Environment, and People*,
7(1), 23. https://doi.org/10.26458/jedep.v7i1.571

Murray, A., & Rawat, D. B. (2021). Network hazard flow for
multi-tiered discriminator analysis enhancement with
systems-theoretic process analysis. *2021 IEEE Global
Humanitarian Technology Conference (GHTC), Global*

Humanitarian Technology Conference (GHTC), 2021 IEEE, 55–61.
https://doi.org/10.1109/GHTC53159.2021.9612416

Nath, A., Rai, S., Bhatnagar, J., & Cooper, C. L. (2024). Coping strategies mediating the effects of job insecurity on subjective well-being, leading to presenteeism: an empirical study. *International Journal of Organizational Analysis (1934-8835), 32*(2), 209–235.
https://doi.org/10.1108/IJOA-10-2022-3476

NIST SP 800-34 | NIST (2021). NIST.
https://www.nist.gov/privacy-framework/nist-sp-800-34

NIST (2021). National Institute of Standards and Technology. *Disaster Resilience Framework*. Retrieved from https://www.nist.gov

NOAA (2022). National Oceanic and Atmospheric Administration. *Historical Hurricane Data*. Retrieved from https://www.noaa.gov

Oyama, Y., Abiru, N., Kit, A., Eyama, D., Noda, A., & Nagata, A. (2021). Thoughts and attitudes toward disasters among Japanese patients with type 1 diabetes: A qualitative descriptive study. *Japan Journal of Nursing Science, 19*(2). https://doi.org/10.1111/jjns.12459

Oyama, T., Okada, N., & Yamaguchi, Y. (2021). Disaster preparedness and resource preservation in SMEs. *Journal of Contingencies and Crisis Management, 29*(1), 25-37.

Palinkas, L. A., Springgate, B. F., Sugarman, O. K., Hancock, J., Wennerstrom, A., Haywood, C., Meyers, D., Johnson, A., Polk, M., Pesson, C. L., Seay, J. E., Stallard, C. N., & Wells, K. B. (2021). A rapid assessment of disaster preparedness needs and resources during the COVID-19 pandemic. *International Journal of Environmental Research and Public Health, 18*(2). https://doi.org/10.3390/ijerph18020425

Pope, D. C. (Academic). (2017). *Introduction to qualitative research methods* [Video]. Sage Research Methods. https://doi.org/10.4135/9781473991958

Pradhan, R. K., Panda, M., Hati, L., Jandu, K., & Mallick, M. (2024). Impact of COVID-19 stress on employee performance and well-being: Role of trust in management and psychological capital. *Journal of Asia Business Studies*, *18*(1), 85–102. https://doi.org/10.1108/JABS-01-2023-0023

Ready.gov. (2023). A ready business: Free disaster preparedness tool provided by Ready.gov. https://www.ready.gov/business

Riaz, R., & Khan, A. (2024). Developing a research design based on the distinction of history from the social sciences. *Journal of Research in Social Sciences*, *12*(1), 1-25. https://doi.org/10.52015/jrss.12i1.236

Ruiz-Cantisani, M. I., Vargas-Florez, J., Castro-Zuluaga, C. A., & Marquez-Gutierrez, M. (2020). SMEs´ Resilience Model based on Maturity Cycle. *Proceedings of the 18th LACCEI International Multi-Conference for Engineering, Education, and Technology: Engineering, Integration, and Alliances for a Sustainable Development" "Hemispheric Cooperation for Competitiveness and Prosperity on a Knowledge-Based Economy."* https://doi.org/10.18687/laccei2020.1.1.304

Saad, M. H., Hagelaar, G., Van Der Velde, G., & Omta, S. (2021). Conceptualization of SMEs' business

resilience: A systematic literature review. *Cogent
Business & Management*, *8*(1).
https://doi.org/10.1080/23311975.2021.1938347

Sadeghi, R. J. K., Azadegan, A., Ojha, D., & Ogden, J. A.
(2022). Benefiting from supplier business continuity:
The role of supplier monitoring and buyer power.
Industrial Marketing Management, *106*, 432–443.
https://doi.org/10.1016/j.indmarman.2022.09.009

Saldaña, J. (2009). *The coding manual for qualitative
researchers*. http://ci.nii.ac.jp/ncid/BB20067005

Saldaña, J. (2014). Coding and analysis strategies. *Coding
and Analysis Strategies*, 580–598.
https://doi.org/10.1093/oxfordhb/9780199811755.013.0
01

Salmia, S. S. (2023). Development of quality instruments and
data collection techniques. *Journal Pendidikan dan
Pengajaran Guru Sekolah Dasar (JPPGuseda)*.

Sarmiento, J. P., Sarmiento, C., Hoberman, G., Jerath, M., &
Sandoval, V. (2019). Small and medium enterprises in
the Americas, the effect of disaster experience on

readiness capabilities. *AD-minister, 35*, 117–136. https://doi.org/10.17230/ad-minister.35.5

Schroeder, T., Haug, M., Georgiou, A., Seaman, K., & Gewald, H. (2024). Evidence of how physicians and their patients adopt mHealth apps in Germany: Exploratory qualitative study. *JMIR mHealth and uHealth, 12.* https://doi.org/10.2196/48345

Serenko, A., Abubakar, A. M., & Bontis, N. (2024). Understanding the drivers of organizational business performance from the human capital perspective. *Knowledge & Process Management, 31*(1), 48–59. https://doi.org/10.1002/kpm.1763

Seong, M., Ryu, D., & Sok, S. (2023). A study on the types of disaster awareness in nursing students: Q methodology. *BMC Nursing, 22*(1), 1–10. https://doi.org/10.1186/s12912-023-01636-8

Shiferaw, R. M., Bogale, A. T., & Debela, K. L. (2022). Implementing research methods with confidence: A review of research methodology: A step-by-step guide for beginners. *The Qualitative Report, 27*(11), 2659-2667. https://doi.org/10.46743/2160-3715/2022.6024

Silva, A. J., & Pinto, D. (2024). Training under an extreme context: The role of organizational support and adaptability on the motivation transfer and performance after training. *Personnel Review.* https://doi.org/10.1108/pr-09-2022-0629

Sou, G., Shaw, D., & Aponte-Gonzalez, F. (2021). A multidimensional framework for disaster recovery: Longitudinal qualitative evidence from Puerto Rican households. *World Development*, p. *144*, N.PAG. https://doi.org/10.1016/j.worlddev.2021.105489

Smith, J., & Anderson, P. (2020). *Disaster Preparedness in Tennessee SMEs*. Business Continuity Journal, 25(4), 45-62.

Stake, R. E. (1978). The case study method in social inquiry. *Educational Researcher*, 7(2), 5–8. https://doi.org/10.3102/0013189x007002005

Shweta, S., Kumar, D., & Chandra, D. (2022). A hybrid framework to model resilience in the generic medicine supply chain of MSMEs. *Benchmarking*, *30*(6), 2189–2224. https://doi.org/10.1108/bij-11-2021-0697

Tennessee. (n.d.). U.S. Small Business Administration. https://www.sba.gov/district/tennessee

Tennessee Emergency Management Agency. (2021). *Annual Report on Disaster Response and Preparedness*. TEMA Publications.

Tkachenko, O., Seo, J., & Ardichvili, A. (2022). Case study research in HRD: a review of trends and call for advancement. *European Journal of Training & Development*, *46*(7/8), 693–708. https://doi.org/10.1108/EJTD-10-2021-0160

Tosun, E., & Bostan, S. (2021). Disaster and emergency preparedness in Istanbul museums. *Museum Management and Curatorship*, *37*(2), 159–178. https://doi.org/10.1080/09647775.2021.1969678

Utami, I. D., Santosa, I., & Rifa'i, E. (2021). Conceptual modeling of resilience measurement during natural disasters for SMEs. *IOP Conference Series*, *1072*(1), 012050. https://doi.org/10.1088/1757-899x/1072/1/012050

Vaismoradi, M., & Snelgrove, S. (2019). Theme development in qualitative content analysis and thematic analysis.

Journal of Nursing Education and Practice, *6*(5). https://doi.org/10.5430/jnep.v6n5p100

Van Brown, B. L. (2020). Disaster research "metrics": Ethical and methodological considerations of researching disaster-affected populations. *American Behavioral Scientist,* 64(8), 1050–1065. https://doi.org/10.1177/0002764220938115

Varga-Florez, J., Cantisani, M. I., Carlos-Zuluaga, C., & Marquez-Gutierrez, M. (2020). Small and medium enterprise-SMEs´ resilience model based on maturity cycle. *Proceedings of the 18th LACCEI international multi-conference for engineering, education, and technology: Engineering, integration, and alliances for sustainable development: Hemispheric cooperation for competitiveness and prosperity on a knowledge-based economy.* https://doi.org/10.18687/laccei2020.1.1.304

Verheul, M. L., & Dückers, M. L. (2020). Defining and operationalizing disaster preparedness in hospitals: A systematic literature review. *Prehospital & Disaster Medicine*, *35*(1), 61–68. https://doi.org/10.1017/S1049023X19005181

Wang, C., Li, P., & Zhao, J. (2022). Applying COR theory in disaster preparedness for SMEs. *Journal of Business and Economics, 65*(3), 345-367.

Wang, F., Su, W., & Ding, H. (2023). Job autonomy and employee strengths use: The roles of work engagement and job insecurity. *Psihologija, 56*(3), 283–303. https://doi.org/10.2298/psi220416004w

Wang, W., Zhang, H., & Gupta, S. (2022). Research on value co-creation elements in full-scene intelligent service. *Data Science and Management, 5*(2), 77–83. https://doi.org/10.1016/j.dsm.2022.05.001

Webb, T. (2024). *Challenges of Sustainability Small Business Owners Faced During the COVID-19 Pandemic* (Order No. 31240844). Available from Dissertations & Theses @ National University. (3064860923). https://go.openathens.net/redirector/nu.edu?url=https://www.proquest.com/dissertations-theses/challenges-sustainability-small-business-owners/docview/3064860923/se-2

Yin, R. K. (2018). *Case study research and applications: Design and methods* (6th ed.). SAGE Publications, Inc.

Yogia, M. A., Syafaruddin, Z., Wahyudi, S., & Suyastri, C. (2024). Tailoring service delivery innovation architecture: A Service-Dominant Logic theory perspective for micro small and medium enterprises. *JEL Classification: M31, O12, O31, 39*(1), 61. https://doi.org/10.56444/mem.v39i1.4298

Yüzlü, M. Y. (2023). Learner agency transforming into autonomy in the discussion skills course via Moodle. *Novitas-ROYAL, 17*(1), 47–61.

Appendix A
Research Instrument

Semi-Structure and Focus Group Interview Questions

1. How is innovative disaster preparedness awareness described within your organization to mitigate potentially disruptive events?

2. What disastrous experience impacts have affected business operations? If so, can you describe how the consequences influenced your perspective on disaster preparedness?

   a. Are there any lessons learned from past experiences or observing other SMEs challenged with disastrous events?

3. How do leaders and incident response workforce in the organization perceive the risks associated with disasters and the need for evolving technologically-driven disaster preparedness?

4. What specific technological barriers are SMEs facing when implementing disaster preparedness measures?

   a. Can you identify any resource constraints hindering the implementation of disaster preparedness solutions?

5. How has the SME owner perceived the role of collaboration with other SMEs or industry networks like suppliers, and have you been part of any collaborative efforts?

6. How are technological measures currently leveraged within the SME for disaster preparedness?

   a. Are there any technological solutions found compelling or challenging to implement?

7. To what extent do SME owners and incident response workforce obtain relevant and trending disaster preparedness training that is innovative and technologically focused?

   a. How can SME owners improve or invest in disaster preparedness training programs using technologically innovative tools for a resilient incident response workforce with robust readiness abilities?

   b. Do SME owners, incident response workforce, and stakeholders believe there should be a need for more accessible, innovatively tailored training resources for all other employees?

8. What innovative mitigatory strategies could contribute to integrating long-term resilience against disruptive events?

The interview questions will be modified to meet the specific context of the SME owners the researcher will be interviewing while encouraging open and honest responses to collect valuable information.